Data-centric Regenerative Built Environment

'Sustainable built environment is one of, if not, the biggest challenges for humankind in our time. Big data offers a unique opportunity to collect and analyse information relating to our urban land use, transportation and traffic, environmental concerns and social issues. Potentially, with access to a mass of data on a scale not previously available, we can optimise the ways our cities function to deliver economic, social and environmental sustainability. In this innovative book, Dr Saeed Banihashemi and Sepideh Zarepour Sohi show us how this regenerative built environment might be achieved through big data technologies and applications.'

Professor Sara Wilkinson, *University of Technology Sydney*

This book examines the use of big data in the regenerative urban environment and how data helps in functional planning and design solutions.

This book is one of the first endeavours to present data-driven methods for regenerative built environments and integrate them with novel design solutions. It looks at four specific areas in which data is used – urban land use, transportation and traffic, environmental concerns and social issues – and draws on the theoretical literature concerning regenerative built environments to explain how the power of big data can achieve the systematic integration of urban design solutions. It then applies an in-depth case study method on Asian metropolises including Beijing and Tehran to bring the developed innovation into a research-led practical context.

This book is a useful reference for anyone interested in driving sustainable regeneration of our urban environments through big data-centric design solutions.

Saeed Banihashemi is Assistant Professor of Built Environment discipline in the School of Design and Built Environment, Faculty of Arts and Design; University of Canberra (UC), Australia. He obtained his PhD from the Built Environment school of University of Technology Sydney (UTS).

Sepideh Zarepour Sohi has a mixed background of urban planning and design, and graduated from the Faculty of Fine Arts, University of Tehran, Iran. She is a professional urban designer and planner.

Routledge Research in Sustainable Planning and Development in Asia
Series Editor: Richard Hu

Urban Flood Risk Management
Looking at Jakarta
Christopher Silver

Data-centric Regenerative Built Environment
Big Data for Sustainable Regeneration
Saeed Banihashemi and Sepideh Zarepour Sohi

For more information about this series, please visit: www.routledge.com/ Routledge-Research-in-Sustainable-Planning-and-Development-in-Asia/ book-series/RRSPDA

Data-centric Regenerative Built Environment

Big Data for Sustainable Regeneration

**Saeed Banihashemi and
Sepideh Zarepour Sohi**

LONDON AND NEW YORK

First published 2022
by Routledge
4 Park Square, Milton Park, Abingdon, Oxon OX14 4RN

and by Routledge
605 Third Avenue, New York, NY 10158

Routledge is an imprint of the Taylor & Francis Group, an informa business

© 2022 Saeed Banihashemi and Sepideh Zarepour Sohi

British Library Cataloguing-in-Publication Data
A catalogue record for this book is available from the British Library

Library of Congress Cataloging-in-Publication Data
Names: Banihashemi, Saeed, 1985- author. | Sohi, Sepideh
   Zarepour, 1987- author.
Title: Data-centric regenerative built environment : big data for
   sustainable regeneration / Saeed Banihashemi and Sepideh
   Zarepour Sohi.
Description: Abingdon, Oxon ; New York, NY : Routledge,
   2022. | Series: Routledge research in sustainable planning and
   development in Asia | Includes bibliographical references and
   index.
Identifiers: LCCN 2021058854 (print) | LCCN 2021058855
   (ebook) | ISBN 9780367689926 (hbk) | ISBN 9780367689933
   (pbk) | ISBN 9781003139942 (ebk)
Subjects: LCSH: Sustainable development—Asia. | City
   planning—Asia—Data processing. | Big data—Asia.
Classification: : LCC HC79.E5 B3495 2022 (print) | LCC HC79.
   E5 (ebook) | DDC 338.9/27095—dc23/eng/20220118
LC record available at https://lccn.loc.gov/2021058854
LC ebook record available at https://lccn.loc.gov/2021058855

ISBN: 978-0-367-68992-6 (hbk)
ISBN: 978-0-367-68993-3 (pbk)
ISBN: 978-1-003-13994-2 (ebk)

DOI: 10.4324/9781003139942

Typeset in Times New Roman
by Apex CoVantage, LLC

Saeed dedicates this book to Shiva, his lovely wife, and his parents, for all their devotions and care.

Sepideh dedicates the book to her family and her husband, Alireza, for their support and encouragement.

Contents

Figures

Tables

Preface

Sustainable urbanization has evolved into a globalized phenomenon, the imperative which strengthens the links and synchronizes the movements among humanity, nature and the economy in our built habitat. However, at this stage of development, sustaining our built environment is considered to be 'not enough'. As a pioneering endeavour though, there is a need to start thinking of regenerative, rather than just sustainable development. There is a need, indeed, to move from a narrow focus on the performance and minimization of impacts, to a broader framework that enriches place, people and ecology at the core of the regenerative design call.

The regenerative process here proceeds from the macro to the micro scale. It starts by reconnecting to the essence of sustainable urbanization, antedated to the perception of human behaviour, patterns, flows and networks, rooted in the interaction of people, space and time. The Big Data technology provides interoperable databases, allowing different data (voluntary, automatic and monitored) to be linked together, which can be a support for regenerative planning and design. However, the implementation of regenerative planning requires a circular approach in monitoring the flows instead of states, and big data, by its very nature, is considered an appropriate tool for this issue. The result can be, therefore, a regenerative urban planning and design which follows conscious processes of learning and participation through action, reflection and dialogue via the data-centric approach.

We, hence, undertake this explanatory approach in order to discover how the data-centric approach can be steered towards sustainable urban planning and design. This is an inexplicable phenomenon that has not been examined clearly and comprehensively so far, while we try to explain how big data will advise and enhance regenerative planning and design outcomes. This commences with extensive research to unfold the concepts and develop the theoretical foundations of the data-centric regenerative built environment. It further conceptualizes its characteristics and elements, introduces resources and technologies for its collective implementation and delivers the application in various urban aspects. The in-depth case study method is, then, conducted to bring the ideas into a research-led practical context. This allows for a greater explanation of the presented framework and detailed analysis of big data technologies through the voice and experience of the actors involved in Asian metropolises including Beijing and Tehran. The book is particularly topical for Asian cities and a prominent contribution in the global context as it addresses the validity of insights into the big data and sustainable built environment.

This initiative looks at urban sustainability regeneration through the technological point of view. We acknowledge the significance and crucial role of policy, governance and regulative practices; however, these areas are not within the scope of this focused book.

The book raises the awareness of big data and its contribution towards the sustainable approach for built environment academics, researchers, students and practitioners. Urban designers and planners, data scientists, smart city experts, urban informatics, policy makers and public and private stakeholders can immensely benefit from the generated knowledge, theory, concepts, findings and discussions.

Global scholarship and readership can be also informed through the comprehensive analysis on the classics of big data in the built environment and the developed concept and approaches in urban land use, traffic and transportation, environmental sustainability and socio-cultural resilience. This is further connected to the Asian context via research-led experiential learnings on case analyses of popular Asian metropolises, reflecting upon presented frameworks, successes, failures, achievements and challenges of big data-integrated urban analysis.

The book can be further taught to and integrated into the curricula of higher education and tertiary institutions in both undergraduate and postgraduate levels in the built environment and data science disciplines (e.g., urban design and planning, architecture, computer science, artificial intelligence). Higher Degree by Research students may find this book valuable and beneficial for literature review, theoretical framework development, research problematization and realizing the big data aspects in sustainable urban environment.

Abbreviations

AHP	Analytical Hierarchy Process
APM	Airborne Particulate Matter
AQCC	Air Pollution Control Department
AQI	Air Quality Index
BTS	Base Transceiver Stations
CCTV	Closed Circuit TV
CDRS	Call Detail Records
DBSCAN	Density-Based Clustering Algorithm
DEM	Digital Elevation Model
DTW	Dynamic Time Warping
END	European Noise Directive
GPS	Global Positioning System
GSI	Ground Space Index
GTWR	Geographically and Temporally Weighted Regression
GWR	Geographically Weighted Regression
IDBSCAN	Improved Density-Based Clustering Application
LBS	Location-Based Service
MPD	Mobile Phone Data
NLP	Natural Language Processing
OLS	Ordinary Least Squares
OSM	Open Street Map
POI	Point of Interest data
SCD	Smart Card Data
SOM	Self-Organizing Maps
SPL	Sound Pressure Level
SPM	Suspended Particulate Matter
STC	Space-Time-Cube
VGI	Volunteered Geographic Information
WSN	Wireless Sensor Network

1 Classics of Data-Centric Regenerative Built Environment

Introduction

Humans and their activities are the focal point of city formation and urban development. Urban growth and development, in addition to providing opportunities for people to have a better life, can create some problems and issues in various aspects if they are not sustainable. As a consequence, it is necessary to develop urban areas in a sustainable manner and meanwhile, regenerate cities to resolve the urban social, economic, physical and environmental problems that are due to uncoordinated growth and development.

With the current technology trends and advent of big data with its three main features of volume, velocity and variety, it is feasible to understand a real perception of patterns of human behaviour from high spatial and temporal resolutions. Understanding the residents' patterns through the main urban environmental, functional, traffic and transportation components, and the social aspects which develop a real-time sustainable city can be immensely effective for the regeneration of urban areas.

This chapter, therefore, theorizes what a data-centric approach entails for the sustainable urban regeneration of these components, how big data can be integrated in the design and planning process and what types of technologies contribute to sustainable urban land use, transportation, environmental and social aspects.

Urban Development and Regeneration

Sustainable development is seminally delineated as the 'development that meets the requirements of the present without compromising the ability of future generations to meet their own needs'. With this respect, sustainable urban development was further coined in the early 1990s after the construction of global industrial cities and permeated into the urban planning principles to get cities and human settlements to become more inclusive,

DOI: 10.4324/9781003139942-1

safe, resilient and sustainable [1]. To address these objectives, sustainable urban development has been directed towards the harmonized development of three fundamental factors of the environment, economy and society [2].

On top of that, urban regeneration seats where the 'regeneration' was first applied by the British Government during the 1970s to launch a new phase of national policies aimed at enhancing the employment of the middle class of workers and, at the same time, resolving their housing issues [3]. The concept of urban regeneration has become progressively a portion of national and local policies for reuse and rectification of the built environment [4] and can be equivalent with urban rehabilitation and urban renovation, as well [5].

The sustainable urban development requires improving strategies to regenerate urban areas. Urban regeneration is, therefore, regarded as a multidisciplinary approach that comprises policy-making and implementation processes in the field of urban planning, urban design, transportation, urban economy, urban development, sustainable solution and housing design [6]. It encompasses the rebirth or renewal of urban areas and settlements where the overall goal is to obtain high quality, well-designed and sustainable places for people to live, work and enjoy. This concept also looks for enhancing people's quality of life in downstream and raising the economic growth in upstream [5, 7]. Moreover, during the process of urban regeneration, it is necessary to have a profound theoretical intuition incorporated with actions to the resolution of urban problems and minimize the harmful effects on the natural environment [8]. It is argued that urban regeneration proposes fundamental opportunities to deliver sustainable cities and achieve sustainable development [5, 9].

The regeneration of urban areas can include various actions such as:

- The renovation of historic regions,
- The improvement of living quality in residential areas,
- The renewal of public spaces including squares and parks,
- The modernization of urban infrastructures such as water networks, gas, electricity and transportation [4].

Big Data Technology

The progress and development of technology has immersed us in a huge amount of data. The age of 'Big Data' is coming and altering our perception from the world [10] as its application is getting more and more popular [11]. Big data was originally introduced by John-Mashey, the retired former chief scientist at Silicon Graphics, to explain the management and analysis of enormous datasets [12]. It is stated that this concept emerged as a term concerning visualization around 20 years ago. 'Visualization implements a new challenge for computer systems: datasets are commonly quite enormous, occupy the capacities of main memory, local disk, and even remote disk. We call this the problem of big data' [13].

There is no specific and agreed formal definition in industry or academia about what is generally intended with the term of big data, same as the many terms applied to advancing technology [11, 14]. But, it is evident that 'Big Data' sets are now applied in different areas such as physics, genomics, industry sectors and government agencies [11].

Big data, as its name proposes, is mainly specified by size or volume [13]. It points to enormous datasets that may be analyzed to disclose patterns, trends, dependencies and principles relating to human behaviour and interactions [10] and unpredictable qualitative and quantitative relationships that would not have been feasible through smaller datasets [11]. Big data also attracts our attention to changes occurring in much smaller time spans [13]. It is connected to structured and unstructured data and spontaneously generated as a part of transactional, operational, planning and social activities [15]. Apparently, it is hard to analyze such volume of data through conventional data-processing methods [16].

TechAmerica Foundation of Federal Big Data Commission defines big data as a term that explains huge volumes of high velocity, complicated and variable data that need advanced techniques and technologies to empower the capture, storage, distribution, management and analysis of the information [17]. From the spatial point of view, Batty describes big data as any data that cannot fit into an Excel spreadsheet and is regularly created in a relation with space and time [18]. In a more ubiquitous definition, IBM, in 2013, characterized big data as a data which originates from everywhere, for instance, from the sensors used to collect climatic information, posts or comments in social media networks, digital pictures and videos, financial transaction records and cell phones GPS signals [17]. In another definition, big data is a term indicating enormous and complicated datasets that need adapting to common approaches or expanding to absolutely new methods for their analysis [16, 19]. Practically speaking, it is stated that if the size of data overpasses the capacities of the standard data management tools, it will be considered as big data [10].

Doug Laney [20] characterizes big data with three main and salient features to distinct it from traditional and small data based on the features of:

- Volume: containing large quantities of data and massive in volume, including terabytes or petabytes of data,
- Velocity: the speed at which data is transferred (created in or near real-time and having temporality),
- Variety: various types of data (structured, semi-structured, non-structured and spatial-temporal datasets).

There are also other attributes to big data including:

- Veracity: this concerns the quality of data which has an influence on the accuracy of analysis and means that data can be messy, noisy and may have faults and uncertainties,
- Variability: data whose meaning can be regularly changing in relation to the context in which they are created and which show an amount of inconsistency,
- Scalability and extensionality: having the flexibility in increasing the size or adding new data fine-grained in resolution, to be as detailed as possible,
- Value: many insights can be obtained,
- Rationality: enabling the inclusion of different datasets [12, 13, 21] (Figure 1.1).

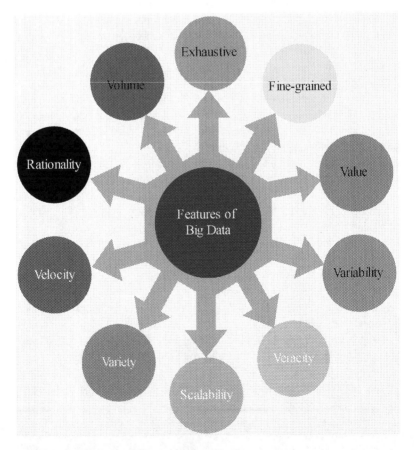

Figure 1.1 Features of big data technology

Tools and Sources of Big Data for Urban Regeneration

In general, human beings play a key role in generating big data. Big data are actually provided through sensors and tools which are available to people. These data can be categorized in three forms of voluntary, automatic and monitored data [14, 21]. Voluntary data includes social media (Twitter, Facebook, etc.) and Volunteered Geographic Information (VGI). Automatic data are produced in two ways: from data sources which are created coincidental to human activities such as Mobile Phone Data (MPD), Smart Card Data (SCD) and Global Positioning System (GPS) data [22, 23], and from sensors and objects which are fixed in the environment and monitor human activities via technologies such as Wireless Sensor Networks (WSN) and Closed Circuit TV (CCTV). In addition to the voluntary and automatic types, monitored data are the third category which are collected and protected by human operators and include administrative/governmental and private sector data [15, 23, 24].

Volunteered Data

Location-Based Social Media Data

The advancement of the internet brings novel opportunities for communication with people through social media data which encompass huge amounts of data about people's behaviour, mobility and feelings about places [25]. In fact, people act as a sensor through smartphones to produce huge amounts of datasets related to urban and social aspects [26]. Data collection for urban analysis through social media does not have limitations of the traditional methods such as long data collection time and identifying geo-location signs. Moreover, intangible aspects of urban life can be explored through information extracted from location-based social media [27] where the social networks generate and disseminate data to other users about what happened, when and where it happened [28].

According to the statistics reported in 2018, the number of active social media users comes near to 3.196 billion [27]. People voluntarily post geo-tagged social media through networks such as Twitter, Instagram and Facebook consisting of semantic and contextual information and the explanation of a specific place, activities and feelings of users in the visual, audio and written formats [21, 29].

Volunteered Geographic Information (VGI)

VGI provides richer and more up-to-date geographic information from cartographic centres and executive organizations [30]. This tool is a remarkable technology for Geographic Information Systems (GIS) and is growing rapidly [31]. It allows users to record and share geographic information in the written forms (their satisfaction from locations, feelings, reluctance and motive of a place) at any time [22]. In fact, this tool creates geographic-spatial information sources through people's personal contributions [32].

Automatic

GPS (Global Positioning System)

Unlike the time-consuming and expensive methods such as household travel surveys, census data and questionnaires in identifying people's mobility patterns, GPS trajectories, with a great level of spatial precision and temporal regularity, can be a wealthy source for discovering mobility patterns and human behaviour and activities in large scale and with deep and accurate means [33, 34].

GPS trajectories data can be collected through two methods: 'on foot' (handheld GPS devices or mobile phones) and 'on ride' vehicles (taxis equipped with GPS) [34]. Among these methods, taxi GPS data is the better choice because of its thorough coverage of the road networks, high level of frequency and easy access [35]. Various information, such as position (latitude and longitude), speed, time, direction of travel, origin and destination, can be extracted from GPS data as well [36]. This dataset can be useful for the analysis of transportation structures, the detection of urban shopping centres, urban traffic forecasts and monitoring, travel demand forecasts, traffic volume simulation, identification of land use patterns and hotspot areas for urban planning [22, 33, 37, 38].

SCD (Smart Card Data)

A smart card is a plastic card similar to credit cards in look and size [39]. It has a computer chip in-fixed and can be categorized in two types of contact or contactless [40]. A smart card is the primary tool for residents for their transportation and for identifying their daily travel records [41].

SCDs, collected by automated fare collection, are precious sources for understanding urban mobility as these are complete, extensive, accurate and real-time data sources about public transport users. The information extracted from SCDs are spatial and temporal which means the time and location of boarding and alighting of each passenger are achieved [42]. In other words, an origin-destination matrix can be conveniently collected from SCDs [43].

These data can be applied in different fields including the analysis of transit riders' travel patterns, performance assessment of bus transport reforms, planning of the public transportation systems [44], activity recognition [45], measuring jobs-housing correlation in urban areas and predicting travel demands [42].

MPD (Mobile Phone Data)

People carry their mobile phone everywhere because it is the central device of communication now. As a result, MPD has become an enormous data source through its diurnal commuting and activities of its users [46]. MPD covers an extensive spatial area and is an economical [47] and trustworthy data source compared to household mobility surveys and road sensors [48].

MPD can be classified into three main categories:

1) CDR (Call Detail Records), which archives time and location of people calling,
2) LBS (Location-Based Service), which records people's movement, flows, and events,
3) Handover data [49].

MPD encompasses a wealth of data which can be applied in various realms like, disclosing people's travel trajectories, exploring the spatial nature of human mobility, helping demographic censuses [50], perceiving home-work locations and commuting patterns [51] and measuring the spatial and temporal variations in urban vibrancy and vitality [47].

Sensors and Objects (Fixed Sensors)

Closed-Circuit Television (CCTV)

CCTV uses video cameras to transfer signals to a specific place with a set of monitors. In fact, CCTV is implemented for surveillance of numerous cameras internally and analyzes produced images to elicit real-time information [52]. Overall, CCTV data comprise events and their sequences, locations of people, material objects and their dynamic variations in the time and space dimensions [53].

Big data analytics from spatially heterogeneous CCTV images can provide fundamental knowledge for traffic behaviour [54], such as traffic parameters including speed, traffic composition, vehicle shapes and types, vehicle identification numbers and incidence of traffic violations or road accidents [52]. Another application of CCTV is crime prevention; it decreases the public fear of crime and assists in better management of social places [55] as evidenced in developed countries such as the U.K, the US and France [56]. CCTV can be installed in various locations such as airports, banks, ATM stations, residential areas, nightclubs and communal buildings, parking lots, public transportation and restaurants for reducing crime and promoting the sense of safety and security [57].

Wireless Sensor Networks (WSNs)

WSNs are fast-evolving technology for collecting data in real time [58]. A WSN consists of many autonomous sensor nodes dispersed in the target controlling area [59–61] with small and low-cost sensors which collect and disseminate environmental data [62]. This type of technology senses all changes in physical parameters and environmental conditions such as temperature and humidity and transfers this information to the remote control centres for analysis and taking required actions [63, 64]. WSNs can be remotely controlled, expanded and easily redeployed and adapt well to mobility [65].

This tool is very effective and functional in obtaining roads and traffic information and has led to more efficient transportation systems. In fact, this tool provides a wireless monitoring system for transport planning, which significantly decreases the cost of communication with the wire [66, 67]. This technology is used to create big data on improving traffic safety, controlling traffic congestion, monitoring road conditions and optimally utilizing roads capacity and reducing cost, time and fuel consumption [68]. It also provides big data by monitoring the amount of noise and air pollution for urban environmental analysis [69]. In addition, it provides data for sensing earthquakes and identifying fires for resilient urban design [63].

Monitored Data

Administrative Data (Governmental Data)

Administrative data are derived from the operation of administrative systems, typically collected and held centrally by public sector agencies [70] and are collected for organizational purposes [71]. Administrative systems such as those used in education, healthcare, taxation, housing and vehicle licensing are the sources of administrative information from registers such as notifications of births, deaths and marriages, electoral registration and enrolment, national censuses as well as information obtained from employment forms [72]. These kinds of data are collected in a relatively inexpensive way and provide comprehensive information to researchers in various areas, including urban social sciences [71] and urban economics [15, 23].

Private Sector Data

Private sectors such as contractors and consultants of governmental agencies and entities collect big data in various ways, including trade transactions and exchanges and registered commercial records, and data obtained from financial and welfare institutions. Such big data can be used by public agencies, developers and researchers in different fields [15, 23].

Table 1.1 and Figure 1.2 summarize these tools and their applications.

Concepts and Classics of Data-Centric Regenerative Built Environment Framework

The progress and development of technology and equipping cities with digital tools, sensors and infrastructures have immersed our built environments in a huge amount of data. This provides a rich flow of information about cities and citizens and offers new urban design solutions in the big data era, as its concepts, tools and sources were discussed in the previous sections. We, therefore, propose this initiative to drive the sustainable regeneration of our urban areas.

Data plays a significant role in planning and design operations, but it also suits the novel methods in how we think of and understand our cities. In fact, big data can be a remarkable reorientation in our classics of thoughts and realization of patterns, behaviour and flows in urban planning and design principles resulting from people, space and time interactions [18], subject to its proper conceptualization and effective application (Figure 1.3).

Furthermore, according to Canter [73] and Golkar [74], a sustainable city can be conceptualized in its balanced view of environmental, functional (land use), traffic and transportation infrastructure and social components (see Figure 1.3).

Due to the fact that big data is human-centric data, it can spark new ideas in the know-how of how voluntary, automatic and monitored big data types are utilized in identifying human behaviour, traffic flows and networks and developing meaningful patterns of human impacts, mobilities and activities in cities [15, 21]. Such an integrative approach leads to achieving a

Table 1.1 Tools and sources of generating big data

	Sources		Tools
Sources and tools for generating big data	Volunteered		Social media VGI
	Automatic	Generating coincidental with human activities	GPS (manual GPS devices and data that are collected through GPS of the floating taxis). SCD MPD
		Sensors and objects embedded in the environment by human beings for collecting human activities and the physical environment data	CCTV WSN
	Monitored	Administrative/government data	– Tax and income data and payments, academic records (academic records, registration and enrolment)
		Private sector data	– Purchase and sale transactions and records – Data of financial and welfare institutions

comprehensive and informed recognition regarding the detailed analysis of cities in terms of their air and noise pollution, land uses, travel behaviour, traffic, social analysis and public spaces (see Figure 1.3). On top of that, smart assessment, appraisal, monitoring and control of semantic, spatial and topological hierarchies of cities are coupled with the strategic planning and design solutions in shifting from unsustainable paradigms in urban development to the more sustainable practices through big data lenses.

However, this procedure is a cycle of endless development and adjustment in the urban context. It necessitates the complex interaction of triple bottom line principles through a continuous supervision and critical appraisal of finding intelligent decisions based on big data collection and analysis [21].

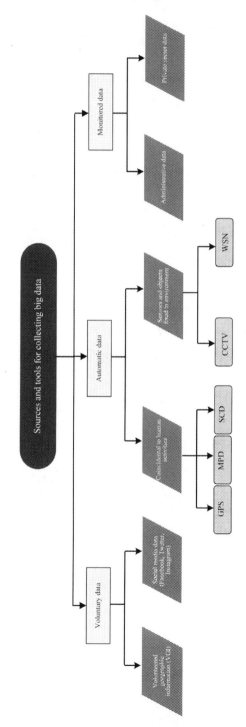

Figure 1.2 Tools and sources of collecting big data

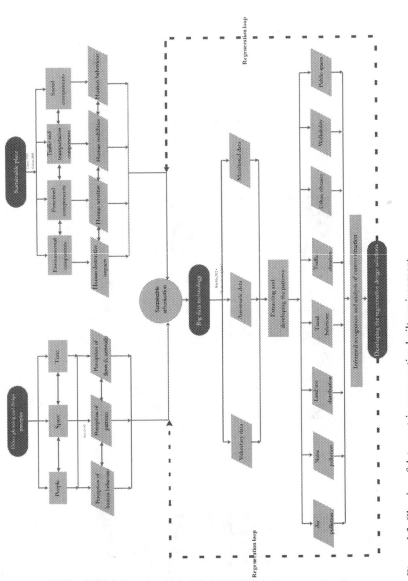

Figure 1.3 Classics of data-centric regenerative built environment

We have, therefore, established the idea and structure of this initiative on the data-centric regenerative built environment as the main and integrated theoretical innovation which is context-free and worthwhile in the international perspective. Progressively, the application and validation of this concept's functional elements are presented through the detailed case studies within the context of major Asian cities. These cities are Beijing, the world's most populous capital city [75] which also represents East Asian megacities, and Tehran, the largest metropolitan area in the Asian Middle East [76]. This book is, hence, structured as follows.

Chapter 2 sets forth the significance of sustainable urban land use planning and conceptualizes the techniques of big data in its regeneration through intelligent classification, monitoring and design procedures. It also provides a detailed perspective on how the technologies of GPS, MPD and social media are integrated and operationalized to exchange and interchange data and enable identification of the land use patterns, zones of residence, work, activity, leisure and tourism and change monitoring. The presented methods and applications are further verified via a research-oriented analysis of Beijing.

Chapter 3 is focused on the evolution of data and its effective integration in the traffic and transportation structure of cities. Acting as the backbone of developing sustainable metropolitan areas, public transportation, traffic control, monitoring and travel behaviour are jointly discussed with big data technology implications. This chapter indicates how big datasets can be developed by a collective integration and dataset interoperability of various technologies such as GPS, SCD, social media, MPD. Traffic and transportation behaviour is then analyzed in the context of Beijing through the taxi GPS trajectories big data source. Hence, the sustainable data-integrated transportation approach is strategized to recognize the locations attracting population and intra-city travels and develop design solutions.

Chapter 4 presents data-enabled methods in urban environmental analysis and examines the major characteristics of spatial and temporal big data collection, along with the principles of how to analyze environmental data they produce. Environmental pollutions, including air and noise pollution, vary widely from place to place and time to time within metropolitan areas, but the patterns of their changes can be conclusively detected and predicted by big data analysis in a variety of ways. Technologies including social media, GPS, MPD and WSN are presented via the integrative groundwork of the data-centric sustainability approach in order to envisage how big data functions in minimizing pollution levels and improving urban sustainability. This discourse is coupled with a case study on Tehran/Iran to conceptualize the application of big data in its urban environmental regeneration.

Chapter 5 indicates social sustainability as one of the main aspects of urban sustainability. In this chapter, big data sources, including social media data and GPS trajectories, are surveyed to analyze vitality and vibrancy as non-physical factors and walkability and well-designed urban public space as physical factors to achieve social sustainability. Following that, social media data are used for regeneration of the urban public space (the case of Bagh Ferdos, Tehran) for enhancing its social sustainability.

Chapter 6 concludes the book with providing an abridged account of the symbiotic nexus of technology and sustainability, contextualized in the data-centric regenerative built environment. This is to authenticate that the mechanics of big data implementation in the urban scope are in line with people-driven and regenerative urban design frameworks. Therefore, the generated knowledge on the theory, concepts, patterns, disciplines, interactions and extractions are summarized, and implications for practice, current limitations as to the reliability, quality and accessibility of big data in the built environment industry are critically presented and recommendations to the future are conferred. Furthermore, the lessons learned from the case implementations of big data in the regenerative design solutions of Beijing and Tehran are explained and the associated challenges, failures, successes and improvement perspectives are outlined, compared and contrasted. In fact, the data-centric approach is viewed in this chapter as a visionary transformer to our built environment, cutting through unsustainable urbanized practices that leave other strategies stranded and link the different layers of planning-centric data to design-led thinking.

References

1   Angelidou, M., et al., Enhancing sustainable urban development through smart city applications. *Journal of Science and Technology Policy Management*, 2018. 9(2): p. 146–169.

2   Yang, B., T. Xu, and L. Shi, Analysis on sustainable urban development levels and trends in China's cities. *Journal of Cleaner Production*, 2017. **141**: p. 868–880.

3   Opoku, A. and J. Akotia, Urban regeneration for sustainable development. *Australasian Journal of Construction Economics and Building*, 2020. **20**(2):1–5.

4   Salata, S. and M. Fior, Urban regeneration: The case study of PORU-Senigallia (Ancona, Italy). *CSE-City Safety Energy*, 2017(1): p. 13–25.

5   Abdo, M.M., et al. Linking urban regeneration to sustainable urban development of smart cities. In *Is This the Real World? Perfect Smart Cities vs. Real Emotional Cities. Proceedings of REAL CORP 2019, 24th International Conference on Urban Development, Regional Planning and Information Society*. 2019. CORP – Competence Center of Urban and Regional Planning.

6   Korkmaz, C. and O. Balaban, Sustainability of urban regeneration in Turkey: Assessing the performance of the North Ankara urban regeneration project. *Habitat International*, 2020. **95**: p. 102081.

7 Handore, K., Urban Regeneration using geo-spatial indicators. *Growth*, 2020. **52**(Part 2).

8 Lak, A., M. Gheitasi, and D.J. Timothy, Urban regeneration through heritage tourism: Cultural policies and strategic management. *Journal of Tourism and Cultural Change*, 2020. **18**(4): p. 386–403.

9 Boyle, L., K. Michell, and F. Viruly, A critique of the application of neighborhood sustainability assessment tools in urban regeneration. *Sustainability*, 2018. **10**(4): p. 1005.

10 Huang, B. and J. Wang, Big spatial data for urban and environmental sustainability. *Geo-Spatial Information Science*, 2020. **23**(2): p. 125–140.

11 Scheutz, M. and T. Mayer, Combining agent-based modeling with big data methods to support architectural and urban design. In *Understanding Complex Urban Systems*. 2016, Springer. p. 15–31.

12 Kitchin, R. and G. McArdle, What makes big data, big data? Exploring the ontological characteristics of 26 datasets. *Big Data & Society*, 2016. **3**(1): p. 2053951716631130.

13 Batty, M., Big data and the city. *Built Environment*, 2016. **42**(3): p. 321–337.

14 Kitchin, R., Big data and human geography: Opportunities, challenges and risks. *Dialogues in Human Geography*, 2013. **3**(3): p. 262–267.

15 Thakuriah, P.V., N.Y. Tilahun, and M. Zellner, Big data and urban informatics: Innovations and challenges to urban planning and knowledge discovery. In *Seeing Cities Through Big Data*. 2017, Springer. p. 11–45.

16 Samarajiva, R., et al., Big data to improve urban planning. *Economic & Political Weekly*, 2015. **50**(22): p. 43.

17 Ma, R., P.T. Lam, and C. Leung. Big data in urban planning practices: Shaping our cities with data. In *Proceedings of the 21st International Symposium on Advancement of Construction Management and Real Estate*. 2018. Springer.

18 Batty, M., Big data, smart cities and city planning. *Dialogues in Human Geography*, 2013. **3**(3): p. 274–279.

19 Chowdhury, P.K.R., et al., 23 Big data in emerging cities. *Big Data for Regional Science*, 2017: p. 277.

20 Laney, D., 3D data management: Controlling data volume, velocity and variety. *META Group Research Note*, 2001. **6**(70): p. 1.

21 Kitchin, R., The real-time city? Big data and smart urbanism. *GeoJournal*, 2014. **79**(1): p. 1–14.

22 Hao, J., J. Zhu, and R. Zhong, The rise of big data on urban studies and planning practices in China: Review and open research issues. *Journal of Urban Management*, 2015. **4**(2): p. 92–124.

23 Ebrahimnia, V. and A. Mahmoudpour. Big data and knowledge-based urban system in Tehran. In *Real Corp 2018 – Expanding Cities – Diminishing Space: Are "Smart Cities" the Solution or Part of the Problem of Continuous Urbanisation Around the Globe? Proceedings of 23rd International Conference on Urban Planning, Regional Development and Information*. 2018. CORP – Competence Center of Urban and Regional Planning.

24 Pan, Y., et al., Urban big data and the development of city intelligence. *Engineering*, 2016. **2**(2): p. 171–178.

25 Nummi, P., Social media data analysis in urban e-planning. *Smart Cities and Smart Spaces: Concepts, Methodologies, Tools, and Applications*, 2019: p. 636–651.

26 Santala, V., et al. Making sense of the city: Exploring the use of social media data for urban planning and place branding. In *Anais Do I Workshop de Computação Urbana*. 2017. SBC.

27 Martí, P., L. Serrano-Estrada, and A. Nolasco-Cirugeda, Social media data: Challenges, opportunities and limitations in urban studies. *Computers, Environment and Urban Systems*, 2019. **74**: p. 161–174.

28 Wu, W., J. Wang, and T. Dai, The geography of cultural ties and human mobility: Big data in urban contexts. *Annals of the American Association of Geographers*, 2016. **106**(3): p. 612–630.

29 Liu, Y., Y. Yuan, and F. Zhang, Mining urban perceptions from social media data. *Journal of Spatial Information Science*, 2020. **2020**(20): p. 51–55.

30 Bégin, D., R. Devillers, and S. Roche, Assessing volunteered geographic information VGI quality based on contributors' mapping behaviours. *International Archives of the Photogrammetry, Remote Sensing and Spatial Information Sciences*, 2013: p. 149–154.

31 Mooney, P., H. Sun, and L. Yan. VGI as a dynamically updating data source in location-based services in urban environments. In *Proceedings of the 2nd International Workshop on Ubiquitous Crowdsourcing*. 2011. ACM.

32 Aragó, P., L. Díaz, and J. Huerta. A quality approach to volunteer geographic information. In *7th International Symposium on Spatial Data Quality (ISSDQ 2011). Raising Awareness of Spatial Data Quality*. 2011.

33 Sadeghinasr, B., A. Akhavan, and Q. Wang, Estimating commuting patterns from high resolution phone GPS data. In *Computing in Civil Engineering 2019: Data, Sensing, and Analytics*. 2019, American Society of Civil Engineers Reston, VA. p. 9–16.

34 Tang, J., et al., Uncovering urban human mobility from large scale taxi GPS data. *Physica A: Statistical Mechanics and Its Applications*, 2015. **438**: p. 140–153.

35 Zhang, K., et al., Analyzing spatiotemporal congestion pattern on urban roads based on taxi GPS data. *Journal of Transport and Land Use*, 2017. **10**(1): p. 675–694.

36 Zhang, H., et al., Detecting taxi travel patterns using GPS trajectory data: A case study of Beijing. *KSCE Journal of Civil Engineering*, 2019. **23**(4): p. 1797–1805.

37 Cao, Y., et al. Tpm: A GPS-based trajectory pattern mining system. In *2019 6th International Conference on Behavioral, Economic and Socio-Cultural Computing (BESC)*. 2019. IEEE.

38 Woodard, D., et al., Predicting travel time reliability using mobile phone GPS data. *Transportation Research Part C: Emerging Technologies*, 2017. **75**: p. 30–44.

39 Bagchi, M. and P. White, What role for smart-card data from bus systems? *Municipal Engineer*, 2004. **157**(1): p. 39–46.

40 Omar, S. and H. Djuhari. Multi-purpose student card system using smart card technology. In *Information Technology Based Proceedings of the Fifth International Conference on Higher Education and Training, 2004. ITHET 2004*. 2004. IEEE.

41 Yu, W., et al., Analysis of space-time variation of passenger flow and commuting characteristics of residents using smart card data of Nanjing metro. *Sustainability*, 2019. **11**(18): p. 4989.

42 Lin, P., et al., Identifying and segmenting commuting behavior patterns based on smart card data and travel survey data. *Sustainability*, 2020. **12**(12): p. 5010.

43 Gong, Y., Y. Lin, and Z. Duan, Exploring the spatiotemporal structure of dynamic urban space using metro smart card records. *Computers, Environment and Urban Systems*, 2017. **64**: p. 169–183.

44 Li, T., et al., Smart card data mining of public transport destination: A literature review. *Information*, 2018. **9**(1): p. 18.

45 Zhou, J., M. Wang, and Y. Long, Big data for intrametropolitan human movement studies: A case study of bus commuters based on smart card data. *International Review for Spatial Planning and Sustainable Development*, 2017. **5**(3): p. 100–115.

46 Bachir, D., et al., Inferring dynamic origin-destination flows by transport mode using mobile phone data. *Transportation Research Part C: Emerging Technologies*, 2019. **101**: p. 254–275.

47 Tang, L., et al., Exploring the influence of urban form on urban vibrancy in Shenzhen based on mobile phone data. *Sustainability*, 2018. **10**(12): p. 4565.

48 Thuillier, E., et al., Clustering weekly patterns of human mobility through mobile phone data. *IEEE Transactions on Mobile Computing*, 2017. **17**(4): p. 817–830.

49 Ghahramani, M., M. Zhou, and G. Wang, Urban sensing based on mobile phone data: Approaches, applications, and challenges. *IEEE/CAA Journal of Automatica Sinica*, 2020. **7**(3): p. 627–637.

50 Song, X., et al., Recovering individual's commute routes based on mobile phone data. *Mobile Information Systems*, 2017. **2017**.

51 Lu, S., et al., Understanding the representativeness of mobile phone location data in characterizing human mobility indicators. *ISPRS International Journal of Geo-Information*, 2017. **6**(1): p. 7.

52 Kurdi, H.A., Review of closed circuit television (CCTV) techniques for vehicles traffic management. *International Journal of Computer Science & Information Technology (IJCSIT) Vol*, 2014. **6**.

53 Socha, R. and B. Kogut, Urban video surveillance as a tool to improve security in public spaces. *Sustainability*, 2020. **12**(15): p. 6210.

54 Peppa, M., et al., Urban traffic flow analysis based on deep learning car detection from CCTV image series. *International Archives of the Photogrammetry, Remote Sensing & Spatial Information Sciences*, 2018. **42**(4).

55 Ashby, M.P., The value of CCTV surveillance cameras as an investigative tool: An empirical analysis. *European Journal on Criminal Policy and Research*, 2017. **23**(3): p. 441–459.

56 Lee, J.Y., K.D. Kim, and K. Kim, A study on improving the location of CCTV cameras for crime prevention through an analysis of population movement patterns using mobile big data. *KSCE Journal of Civil Engineering*, 2019. **23**(1): p. 376–387.

57 Farinmade, A.A., O.A. Soyinka, and K.W.M. Siu, Urban safety and security in Lagos metropolis, Nigeria: CCTV inclusive design for sustainable urban

development. In *Handbook of Research on Urban Governance and Management in the Developing World*. 2018, IGI Global. p. 193–206.

58 Hejlová, V. and V. Voženílek, Wireless sensor network components for air pollution monitoring in the urban environment: Criteria and analysis for their selection. *Wireless Sensor Network*, 2013. **5**(12): p. 229.

59 Micek, J. and J. Kapitulik. Wireless sensors networks in road transportation applications. In *Perspective Technologies and Methods in MEMS Design*. 2011. IEEE.

60 Tajne, K., S. Rathore, and G. Asutkar, Monitoring of air pollution using wireless sensors: A case study of monitoring air pollution in Nagpur city. *International Journal of Environmental Sciences*, 2011. **2**(2): p. 829–838.

61 Swagarya, G., S. Kaijage, and R.S. Sinde, A survey on wireless sensor networks application for air pollution monitoring. *International Journal of Engineering and Computer Science*, 2014. **3**(5): p. 5975–5979.

62 Mujawar, T., V. Bachuwar, and S. Suryavanshi, Air pollution monitoring system in Solapur city using wireless sensor network. *Proceedings Published by International Journal of Computer Applications®(IJCA), CCSN-2013 (1)*, 2013: p. 11–15.

63 Khanafer, M., *Design of efficient mac protocols for IEEE 802.15. 4-based wireless sensor networks*. 2012, Université d'Ottawa/University of Ottawa.

64 Rashid, B. and M.H. Rehmani, Applications of wireless sensor networks for urban areas: A survey. *Journal of Network and Computer Applications*, 2016. **60**: p. 192–219.

65 Mansour, S., et al. Wireless sensor network-based air quality monitoring system. In *2014 International Conference on Computing, Networking and Communications (ICNC)*. 2014. IEEE.

66 Lee, J., et al., Low-cost and energy-saving wireless sensor network for real-time urban mobility monitoring system. *Journal of Sensors*, 2015. **2015**.

67 Hu, X., L. Yang, and W. Xiong, A novel wireless sensor network frame for urban transportation. *IEEE Internet of Things Journal*, 2015. **2**(6): p. 586–595.

68 Kafi, M.A., et al., A study of wireless sensor networks for urban traffic monitoring: Applications and architectures. *Procedia Computer Science*, 2013. **19**: p. 617–626.

69 Gubbi, J., et al. A pilot study of urban noise monitoring architecture using wireless sensor networks. In *2013 International Conference on Advances in Computing, Communications and Informatics (ICACCI)*. 2013. IEEE.

70 Lyon, F., et al., Opening access to administrative data for evaluating public services: The case of the Justice Data Lab. *Evaluation*, 2015. **21**(2): p. 232–247.

71 Playford, C.J., et al., Administrative social science data: The challenge of reproducible research. *Big Data & Society*, 2016. **3**(2): p. 2053951716684143.

72 Connelly, R., et al., The role of administrative data in the big data revolution in social science research. *Social Science Research*, 2016. **59**: p. 1–12.

73 Canter, D., *The psychology of place*. 1977, Manhattan, New York City: St Martin's Press.

74 Golkar, K., *Creating sustainable places, ideas revolving the urban design theory*. 2009, Tehran, Iran: Shahid Beheshti University (SBU).

75 WorldAtlas. *The world's most populated capital cities*. 2018 [cited 2020 30/06]; Available from: www.worldatlas.com/articles/the-world-s-most-populated-capital-cities.html.

76 WorldAtlas. *The 150 largest cities in the world*. 2018 [cited 2020 30/06]; Available from: www.worldatlas.com/citypops.htm.

2 Big Data in Urban Land Use Regeneration

Urban Land Use and Its Significance in Sustainable Urban Planning

Land is considered as one of the limited and important natural resources [1, 2]. It can have various definitions, such as terra firma, the solid earth or solid ground underneath our feet, or the properties which are bought, sold and/or used [3].

Land use concept in urban planning refers to the lands and water areas which are possessed or used in light of human activities [4]. In fact, the natural potential of lands in interaction with cultural backgrounds and physical needs of the society generate the various land use concepts [5]. It is generally argued that the predominant use of land is through the urbanization process [2], which affects economic, social and ecological development and shapes the well-being and quality of life of citizens [6, 7]. However, in contrast to the positive aspects of urban land use, rapid urbanization and the resulting chaotic and unplanned growth of land uses lead to significant environmental deterioration, including the destruction of arable agricultural lands, filling of lowlands, land erosion, cutting of hills and deforestation, uncountable losses of natural resources [8] and social problems [2].

It can be said that anthropogenic pressures and the unprecedented growth of urbanization have made the land into a scarce resource [6, 9] and this trend has imposed great pressures on these resources so far [10]. As a consequence, urban sustainability is severely endangered, while in this dire situation, it is necessary to apply sustainable land use planning principles as one of the most significant prerequisites of urban sustainable development [11].

Holistically, sustainable land use is coordinating the relationship between people and land resources to provide requirements for peoples' lives and future generations' survival in the order of the regeneration, utilization, protection and management of land resources [12]. Particularly, sustainable land use planning is the influential and technical approach in design and control of urban environments [13] to achieve the sustainable physical

DOI: 10.4324/9781003139942-2

development and regeneration [4]. It is believed that through this process, lands can be allocated to various public interests for creating the balance between social, economic and environmental objectives [11, 14]. In other words, designing, organizing and managing mechanisms are carried out through this planning regime to control the existing or new land uses with different purposes [14].

Urban land use planning can be progressed based on the urban land suitability analysis [15]. In fact, the most suitable spatial patterns of future land uses can be determined through the process of land suitability analysis [16]. This is the procedure of characterizing the land tract for specific uses, based on particular requirements and priorities of factors such as safety, comfort and convenience [17]. Through this approach, urban land use planning is developed in terms of established criteria [18].

Most recently, in light of the fact that data science is fast growing, spatial behaviours of urban residents and spatial patterns of urban activities can be analyzed through big data technologies in real time [19]. Hence, spatial land use planning, as the first step, can be conducted through data-driven land suitability analysis to make sustainable use of land resources in the accelerated development of industrialization and urbanization.

Current Situation of Spatial Patterns of Urban Land Use

In order to perform urban land suitability analysis, it is imperative to achieve accurate and up-to-date information on the current land use situation and the spatial pattern of urban activities and how they change. This issue necessitates the substantial data required for urban designers, planners and policy makers [20].

However, though extracting the detailed current situation of urban land use is an essential aspect of urban planning, it is a difficult task [21]. Traditionally, this task was done through manual methods like on-site investigations, direct observations, surveys and questionnaires with efforts to capture how citizens interact with their urban environment [13, 22]. It is clear that this approach not only needs intensive labour sources, but it is also costly, time-consuming and limited to a small number of human subjects where citizens, sometimes, resist providing information [23, 24]. In addition, the manual methods highly depend on the familiarity of surveyors with investigated areas and their personal and physical presence in the investigation [25, 26].

In recent decades, with the advent of the advanced spatial data technologies, satellite data has substituted the traditional approach in extracting the current situation of urban land use patterns via remote sensing technique [27]. It is feasible to discover land use patterns through the remote sensing data, in less time, at lower cost, better accuracy resolution and in real time compared with traditional methods [1, 28]. Land use types can be categorized by this method in a large scale [29]. Likewise, physical characteristics of land use, such as spectral, shape and texture features, are captured [21, 30].

However, this technology has limitations in extracting the human socio-economic functions through remote sensing [31, 32] and this limitation means that the land usage is hard to be solely distinguished from its physical characteristics, especially in a mixed urban area [24]. Since images obtained from remote sensing technique are not taken continuously, it fails to collect real-time data [13]. Moreover, this method is not appropriate to land use analysis in urban regions as the categorization outcomes are significantly correlated with image resolutions, information extraction accuracy and sensor features [23].

In contrast to the remote sensing data which is functional in discovering the land cover and its natural-physical characteristics such as agriculture, forest, grass and wetland areas, there is an emerging type of big data technology: social sensing. This technology applies geo-tagged social media, taxi GPS trajectories and MPD to identify the socioeconomic features of land and to reveal the land uses [33]. Such a collective approach delivers valuable information on human mobility, behaviour and activity patterns [23]. By doing so, it characterizes the social functions of urban land uses and indoor human socioeconomic layers such as commercial, residential, cultural and official [21, 30]. This reveals the urban land use patterns and intra-city functions [31] at higher spatial and temporal resolutions [24, 32, 34, 35]. Hence, the useful information on actual land use patterns are added on, to complement the traditional survey and remote sensing data collections [24, 36]. Figure 2.1 summarizes the positive and negative aspects of these three methods for collecting spatial patterns of urban land uses. It can be concluded that spatial distribution and patterns of the activities happening in urban spaces can be revealed in real time via these technologies.

Data-Centric Land Use Patterns

This section explains different urban land use patterns and the relevant big data sources. Technologies, including taxi GPS trajectories data, geo-tagged social media and MPDs, are presented and their technical processes, advantages and challenges in eliciting the land use patterns are analyzed.

Taxi GPS Trajectories Data

Taxi GPS trajectories provide information for disclosing mobilities, human behaviour and activities patterns in light of the coverage of road networks [37, 38]. Thanks to the fact that spatial and temporal patterns of urban

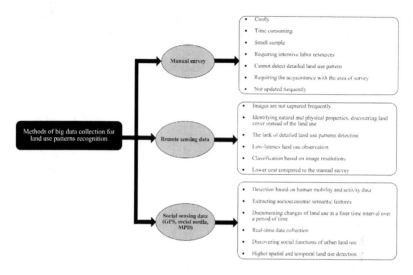

Figure 2.1 Methods of data collection for land use patterns recognition

population flows are considerably reflected by taxi trajectory data, GPS-equipped taxis can be applied as one of the main tools for collecting data in order to characterize land use patterns and discover urban functional areas [39–41]. Generally, it is stated that there is a correlation between taxi GPS data (travel behaviour of people) and social functions of urban areas [40, 42].

Taxi trajectory data typically include the following features:

- Taxi ID,
- Start and end point location (geographic coordinates; latitude and longitude),
- Pick-up and drop-off points,
- Timestamps (start and end time),
- Taxi occupancy status (vacant or occupied).

The analysis of taxi GPS trajectories data has a clear process in which get on/off information from the taxi traces illustrates human mobility characteristics data. It is believed that various locations and land uses distinguish traffic patterns which are discovered in taxi pick-ups and drop-offs [43]. As a result, first, pick-up and drop-off points of certain numbers of taxis are counted in order to discover the regions with specific functions. This means that areas with various social functions (residential, commercial, official) demonstrate diverse patterns of pick-up and drop-off [42].

Afterward, these points are clustered on weekdays and weekends through algorithms such as DTW (dynamic time warping), DBSCAN (a Density-Based Clustering Algorithm), k-means, k-medoids and IDBSCAN (Improved Density-Based Clustering Application) to figure out regions with distinct functions. Accordingly, the boundaries regions with different functions are estimated based on the similarity of the time series of pick-up and drop-off points. In this stage, the differences in urban land use types are specified [41], but the respected functions are still undefined.

Progressively, selected regions are labelled and annotated semantically with various methods such as:

- Point of Interest (POI) data [40, 41, 44],
- Geographic coordinates of Flickr photos (computing functional weight of photos) [39],
- Manual labelling from asking experienced drivers [21, 42, 45].

Following that, the labelled regions are classified based on the pre-defined land use categories like scenic spots; train/coach stations; residential, commercial, educational, recreational, institutional and entertainment districts [42]. Finally, the obtained land use classification is compared with ground truth maps [39] or Google Earth images, Gaode Maps, real photos of landmark areas [41] or local people's labels [40] for validating the accuracy of the developed land use map.

The application of the taxi trajectories data has numerous benefits for revealing urban functional areas:

- It facilitates learning and identification of the dynamic of cities and developing more accurate urban planning for authorities as its recognition accuracy is estimated around +90% [42],
- Cities' land use maps can be regularly updated by this approach and it is feasible to find the important functions that cannot be discovered by other tools [39],
- This approach is a useful guide for people to choose a suitable location for businesses and marketing [39, 40],
- Local people can find city regions having a similarity in functions [40].

Besides the advantages in using taxi GPS trajectories land use patterns, applying this approach has some challenges too:

- GPS taxi trajectories do not cover all parts of the urban area in most cities; these are sparse and have fewer passengers in some areas, and so, urban functional areas cannot be discovered definitely [21, 39],

- Mixed land use areas cannot be perceived by this approach and only regions with mono land uses can be identified [21],
- In some situations, pick-ups and drop-off points of taxi trips are not the first origin or the destination and those are just transition points. Therefore, they cannot present the real land uses [43].

Ultimately, although there are some challenges that urban planners and designers encounter in applying the taxi GPS trajectories data, explicit patterns of urban land uses can be detected and illustrated in timely fashion [40]. It is anticipated that further detailed and reliable urban land use classifications can be identified with improving the processing techniques of this technology in the future [39].

Geo-Tagged Social Media

Geo-tagged social media are another form of big data technology, utilized for identification of urban land uses, which are the supplementary sources of information for urban land use planning objectives. Since the traces of people's interaction with the urban environment can be pursued with social media data, it is beneficial for the automatic characterization of urban functional regions [13]. Social media data for recognizing urban land uses have features including:

- Location GPS coordinates (longitude and latitude),
- Time of the posts (time stamped),
- Status text of users and their posts.

Urban land use patterns resulting from social media data, such as from Twitter, Sina Weibo (a Chinese social media) and Foursquare, can be identified by the following mechanism. Firstly, an urban region is separated into cells through different methods such as grid-based aggregation [23, 46, 47] or Self-Organizing Maps (SOM) [13], to locate social media messages such as Twitter activities in the map. Then, cells with located social media messages (check-in data) are classified through the clustering algorithms such as k-means, DBSCAN and spectral clustering based on similar temporal patterns during weekdays and weekends [13, 23, 46, 47]. After that, through the temporal coherence (the aggregation of social media posts over a long term to demonstrate the time of the day that is associated with each land use) [24], the obtained clusters are labelled based on the pre-defined categories (residential, educational, commercial, business, work area, transportation area, mix land uses, open spaces, recreational). Finally, different methods such as text mining and word clouds [20, 46], using POI data [47,

48] or comparing with ground truth maps and official land use information are applied for the validation of achieved classifications [13, 23].

The identified land use types in the urban area via the geo-tagged social media check-in data benefit from the following:

- It is low-cost to run, relatively simple to apply [46] and a conveniently expandable approach [49],
- It helps discovering the land use patterns in extraordinary spatial resolutions [24] via detailed classification information [23],
- The patterns can be conveniently obtained based on textual data, besides from physical location of land uses [23],
- Identification and awareness of neighbourhoods, city centres and new types of activities such as night life are made [13],
- Urban planners and designers find urban structures in a more detailed scale for urban development requirements [48].

There are some challenges for using the social media messages, though:

- Privacy constraint is one of the main limitations with social media messages [49],
- Land use patterns, in regions which do not have a high density of social media check-in data, cannot be recognized [13],
- Some land use types such as industrial and manufacturing cannot be distinguished due to their scarce check-in data [23].

It can be stated that geo-referenced social media data not only provide the location of activities but also include semantic information such as texts, pictures and voice data [50]. Therefore, geo-tagged social media comprise both spatial and semantic data for land use unlike the taxi GPS trajectories data, which only provide spatial information.

Mobile Phone Data and Call Detail Records

The wide use of smartphones equipped with GPS provides opportunities to collect massive and valuable amount of spatiotemporal datasets through mobile call activities (CDRS) and elicitation of call patterns [51]. These type of data can be applied for extracting urban functional regions and categorizing land use types [52].

MPD and call detail records are collected by Base Transceiver Stations (BTS) towers which are dispersed in urban areas and in the specific period of time during weekdays and weekends. The features, including telephone number, origin and destination, date and time and duration of calls, are extracted from the obtained data [52].

Realizing land use patterns via MPD technology includes the following steps. First, the study area is divided through an approach such as Voronoi Tessellation in which each area is covered by BTS [30, 33, 52–54]. Time series of each BTS activity (calls, messages) are accumulated to infer the land use type. The clustering algorithms such as k-means [52, 53, 55] or fuzzy c-means [30, 54] are then applied to categorize the signals coming from BTS and based on time similarities during weekdays and weekends. Following that, the developed clusters are labelled based on the temporal distribution and intensity of peak time of activities. For instance, the cluster which has two significant peak activities from 8–11 AM and 2–4 PM during the weekdays and a drop at a similar time on weekends can be identified as office areas [55]. As another example, the cluster which has the weekends' activity records as double as those on weekdays or more frequent activities from 12 PM to 5 PM in weekends, can be considered as leisure areas [53].

Finally, the developed patterns are validated through comparison with existing land use maps prepared by authorities [30, 52], ground truth maps (choosing the land mark for comparison) [51, 53–55] and/or using POI data [33, 55].

There are advantages in using MPD for investigating land use patterns:

- Data collection with MPD is low-cost and in real time as compared to manual surveys [52, 53],
- This method is suitable for developing countries which do not have a land use survey but sufficient coverage of mobile phones [33],
- Spatial city structures (monocentric and polycentric) can be revealed by the land use patterns resulting from MPD [52, 55].

But, applying MPD has also challenges:

- It is necessary to try various clustering algorithms and validation mechanisms to verify the accuracy of the land use classification [52],
- In some situations, the land use deduced from MPD has a discrepancy with the description of land use in urban planning [30],
- The precision of land use patterns depends on the density of BTS in that region [30],
- This method can be applied to recognize the land use of the regions which have a specific function and it is not suitable for regions with mixed land uses [54].

As a whole, MPD provides an opportunity to extract the land uses through spatiotemporal data related to human mobility and in high precision. But this approach, because of its challenges, can be more considered as a complementary source for the other methods [52].

Summary

All in all, taxi GPS trajectories, social media data and MPD can be considered as technological approaches for identifying land use patterns. Taxi GPS trajectories and MPD present spatial and temporal information driven by human activities whereas descriptive data can be added to the package through geo-tagged social media. During the process of these three technologies, urban land use patterns are recognized based on the time similarities of received data and their validated methods (see Table 2.1 and Figure 2.2). Although these types of data have some limitations and drawbacks, these are directed towards identifying human behaviour and activities and so, can be considered as reliable and precise sources for developing land use patterns and their regeneration.

Urban Land Use Regeneration of Beijing

Background

Beijing's metropolitan area, the national political capital of China and the world's most populous capital city [56], is located in the north-east of the China Plain [57]. Beijing's urbanization has been growing rapidly as a consequence of performing the economic Reform and the Open Door Policy in 1978 [58]. Hence, both population and urban constructions have experienced unprecedented growth in the last decades. This issue has led to significant changes in urban land uses [59] which creates multiple challenges for its planning in both spatial and functional developments [60].

In this section, the distribution of urban amenities for residential areas of Beijing is analyzed by spatial land use planning (land suitability analysis). Three types of land uses which serve residents, including educational (primary school), healthcare and green space, were selected for analysis.

Educational land use is one of the indispensable urban services which must be supplied for inhabitants. Between the various levels of educational services, primary school is chosen because of its importance in strengthening the identity and social life of a neighbourhood. In other words, it can be stated that primary schools are the central point of neighbourhoods for the creation of communities, prosperity and development of a city, as for

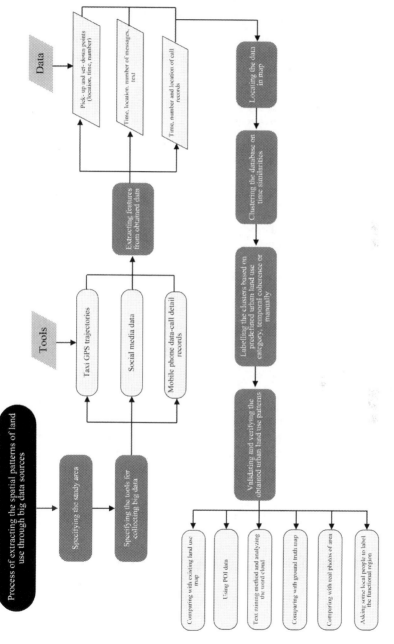

Figure 2.2 The process of identifying land use patterns via taxi GPS data, social media data and MPD

Table 2.1 Big data collection tools and attributes for urban land use patterns

Tools	Taxi GPS trajectories	Geo-tagged social media data	MPD
Type of data	Spatial, temporal	Spatial, temporal, descriptive	Spatial, temporal
Features extracted	• Time of pick-up and drop-off points • Location of pick-up and set-down • Number of pick-up and set-down posts	• Time and location of posts • Number of posts • Text and content of posts	• Time and location of call detail records (calls and messages)
Methodology for processing data	Clustering data based on time similarities and validation		

enhancing its social and economic sustainability by consolidating the culture of communities and residents' literacy [61].

Urban green space was also chosen because green amenities alleviate the destructive environmental impacts of urbanization such as traffic congestion, air and noise pollutions and provide a space for dwellers to have interactions with society [62]. Furthermore, urban green spaces also help people have physical activities and improve their health in both mental and physical aspects [63].

The third urban land use analysis for Beijing focuses on healthcare facilities, which are one of the most fundamental urban services for improving the quality of life and community health [64]. Ensuring people's health with equal access for all residents to healthcare facilities including hospitals can be effective for achieving a healthy society with healthy people. Therefore, a balanced distribution of these urban services is pursued here to enhance the regenerative social, environmental and economic sustainability of Beijing.

Big Data Sources

Social Media Data

Urban land use patterns were extracted from the geo-located Beijing check-in records and from Sina Weibo (a Chinese social media and counterpart of Twitter) and their POI data from 2013[1] records. All 14,357 Beijing check-in records are in the format of points and have attributes including the category and title of the land uses, check-in numbers, latitudes and longitudes of each point. Spatial patterns and distributions of Beijing's people activities such as primary schools, universities, green spaces, hospitals, residential areas, cinemas and theatres are illustrated through POI data, attached to the Sina Weibo check-in data. The density of each activity is then reflected through a number of relevant points and the associated check-in numbers in each ID.

Open Street Map Road Network

The road network data of Beijing was used from the Open Street Map (OSM) network and were downloaded from the same source.[1] The main features used for the data analysis were the type of roads and hierarchy of their networks.

Digital Elevation Model

The Digital Elevation Model (DEM) of Beijing[2] was applied to discover the physical features including the elevation and slope (Table 2.2).

Methodology and Process of Data Analysis

Beijing's land use regeneration through land suitability analysis and big data sources were performed based on the following steps. The criteria of land suitability analysis for choosing the best places of educational (primary schools), medical centres (hospitals) and green space land uses were, first, determined based on the literature and availability of data (Table 2.3). In parallel, big data sources, including social media data, POI, OSM and digital elevation models of Beijing, were applied for analyzing the existing situation based on the defined criteria and ArcGIS 10.7.1 software application.

Table 2.2 Big data sources for urban land use regeneration of Beijing

Big data sources	Types of data	The features	Source of data
Social media data	Distribution and density of urban land use and their classification	Type of activities, Number of check-in data	Beijing City Lab, 2014, Data 24, Beijing check-in records from Sina Weibo www.beijingcitylab.com
OSM	Road networks	Type of roads, Hierarchy of road networks	Beijing City Lab, 2013, Data 12, Open Street Map Beijing 2013 www.beijingcitylab.com
DEM	Slope and elevation	Elevation codes	www.usgs.gov

The spatial land use planning was done through ArcGIS analysis which is one of the popular tools for spatial decision-making [65].

The spatial analysis tools of ArcGIS, applied for recognizing the existing land uses of Beijing, are:

- Distance (Euclidean distance), to measure the distance from different land uses,
- Surface (slope), for measuring the slope,
- Network analysis, to analyze service areas of each land use,
- Hotspot analysis, for recognizing the residential regions with high density areas,
- Spatial analysis (Map algebra), to identify suitable lands for positioning land uses.

Afterwards, the criteria maps, created through identifying the existing situation, needed to be analyzed through the reclassification of each map based on their importance. Through the reclassification process, the current planning land uses were reclassified in three categories as suitable, less suitable and not suitable, which collectively indicate the best places for positioning new land uses.

In line with that, Analytical Hierarchy Process (AHP)[3] as a multi-criteria decision-making analysis was applied to weight each criterion. A pairwise comparison matrix was created, and the criteria weights were computed for each criterion on the scale from 1 to 9, relative to its significance. The ratios of weights were determined according to experts' viewpoints based on the importance of these criteria and their effects on the spatial land use planning.

Next to the weight evaluation of each criterion, the final suitability map for each land use (primary schools, hospitals, green spaces) was created through overlaying the criterion maps and obtained weights. This function was done via the spatial analyst tool Map algebra.

Finally, by comparing and overlaying the final suitability maps and the maps illustrating the regions which lack primary schools, hospitals and green spaces, the suitable regions for locating new primary schools, hospitals and green spaces can be proposed. Figure 2.3 illustrates the process of data analysis for spatial land use planning with big data sources.

Data Analysis and Results

Based on the land use data and activity patterns analysis, the significant criteria related to the urban land use including distances from historical-cultural attractions, commercial areas, existing parks, educational areas, fire stations and high-populated residential areas were calculated. Geo-physical criteria like slope and elevation were then analyzed with DEM and the distance from

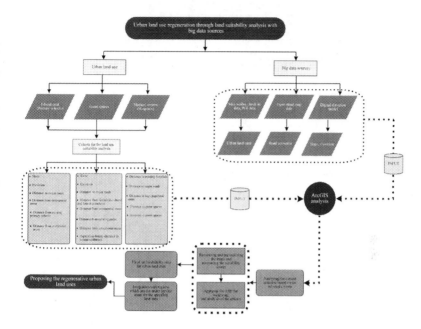

Figure 2.3 The process of data analysis for spatial land use planning with big data sources

major roads was surveyed through OSM for analyzing accessibility and calculating the service areas of each land use. As explained previously, the criteria were further analyzed and reclassified based on the determined distances for each land use (Table 2.3). Figures 2.4, 2.5 and 2.6 illustrate the spatial distributions of green spaces, hospitals and primary schools, the relevant urban service areas and the reclassification of chosen criteria, respectively.

The applied criteria for site suitability selection of green spaces were (Table 2.3):

- Slope and elevation,
    - Generally speaking, the suitable areas for developing green spaces are the areas with the low slope [66].
- Distance from road,
    - It is recommended that green spaces be positioned in the acceptable distance from roads to have a convenient access to transportation [66, 67].

Table 2.3 Criteria of the land suitability analysis for green spaces

Land use	Criterion	Reference	Reclass	Level of suitability
Green space	Slope	[80]	<5 degree	Suitable
			5–15 degree	Less suitable
			>15 degree	Not suitable
	Elevation		<50 m	Suitable
			50–100 m	Less suitable
			>100 m	Not suitable
	Distance from road	[81]	0–100	Suitable
			100–200	Less suitable
			>200	Not suitable
	Distance from historical-cultural and attractions	[82, 83]	<3000 m	Suitable
			3000–6000 m	Less suitable
			>6000 m	Not suitable
	Distance from commercial areas	[84]	<1000 m	Suitable
			1000–2000 m	Less suitable
			>2000 m	Not suitable
	Distance from existing park	[82]	<1500 m	Not suitable
			1500–6000 m	Less suitable
			>6000 m	Suitable
	Distance form educational areas	[81]	0–200 m	Suitable
			200–400 m	Less suitable
			>400 m	Not suitable
	Population-density distance to human settlement	[81]	0–200 m	Suitable
			200–400 m	Less suitable
			400–500	Not suitable

- Distance from historical-cultural attractions,
  - Keeping open green spaces in the vicinity of historical places has an effective role in the conservation of historical areas for future generations [67, 68] and their natural values [69].

- Distance from commercial areas,
  - It is suggested that the regions which are in the proximity of commercial areas are considered as suitable location for positioning green spaces [70].

- Distance from existing park,
  - The regions, which are far from the existing parks, need the green spaces [69].

- Distance from educational areas,
  - The proximity of educational land uses to green spaces [71] create the healthy environment for pupils and teachers [15].

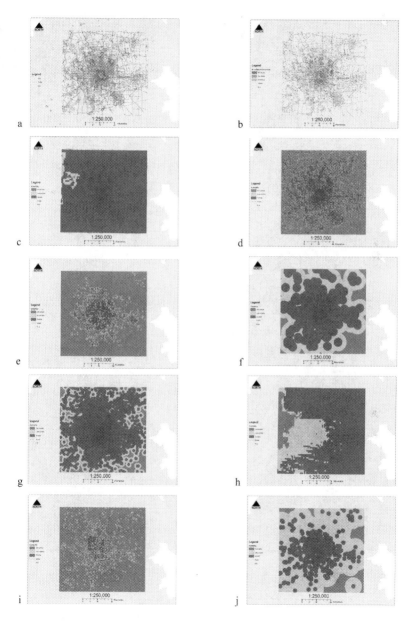

Figure 2.4 a) spatial distribution of existing green spaces. B) green space service areas. c) reclassed slope. d) reclassed distance from roads. e) reclassed distance from residential areas. f) reclassed distance from historical areas. g) reclassed distance from commercial areas. h) reclassed elevation. i) reclassed distance from educational areas. j) reclassed distance from existing green spaces

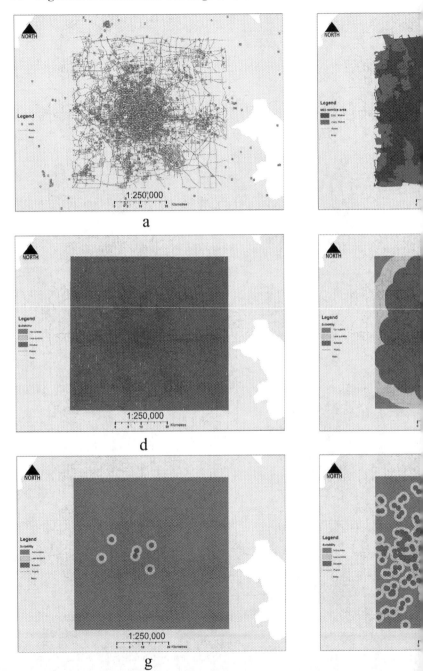

Figure 2.5 a) spatial distribution of existing hospitals. b) service areas of existing hospitals. c) high populated and low populated residential areas. d) reclassed slope. e) reclassed distance from high populated area.

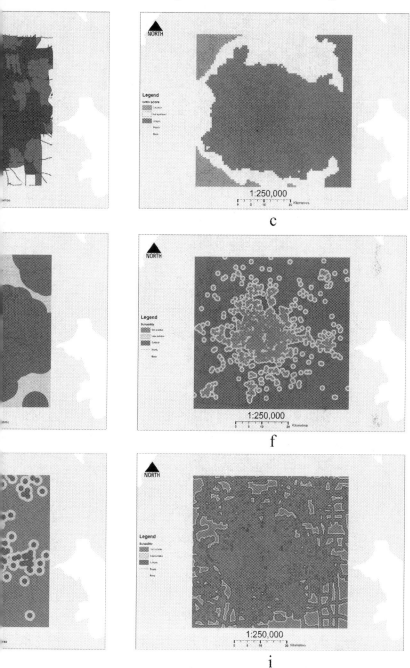

f) reclassed distance from green space. g) reclassed distance from exiting fire stations. h) reclassed distance from existing green space. i) distance from existing major roads

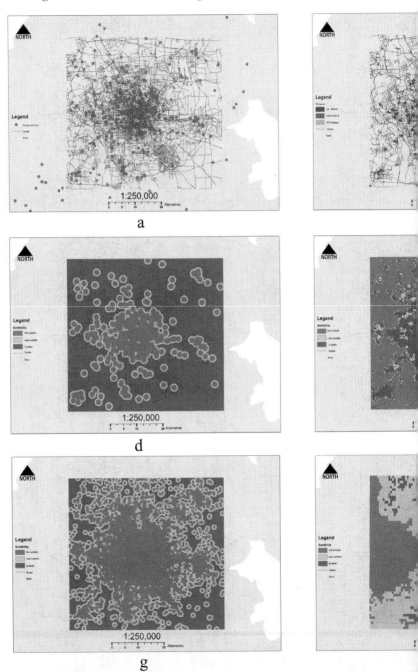

Figure 2.6 a) spatial distribution of primary schools. b) service areas of primary
schools. c) service areas of residential regions. d) reclassed distance
from existing primary schools. e) reclassed distance from residential

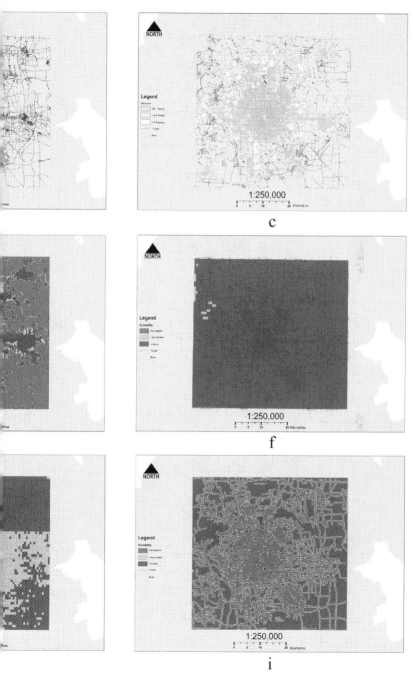

areas. f) reclassed slope. g) reclassed distance from commercial areas.
h) reclassed DEM. i) reclassed distance from major roads

- Distance from high-density residential areas,

    - The regions which are in the proximity of dense populated areas are suitable for locating green spaces [72].

The applied criteria for healthcare site selection were (Table 2.4):

- Distance from existing hospitals and healthcare centres,

    - It is necessary to locate new hospitals and healthcare centres in places which lack medical centres [73].

- Distance from major roads,

    - It is important that cars and emergency services have a convenient access to hospitals and medical centres. Hence, the adjacency of healthcare facilities to major roads is a fundamental criterion to locate hospitals [74].

- Adjacency to densely residential areas,

    - Healthcare centres should be located in the proximity of dense populated regions [75].

Table 2.4 Criteria of the land suitability analysis of hospitals

Land use	Criteria	Reference	Reclass	Level of suitability
Hospital	Distance to existing hospitals and medical centres	[85]	<500 m 500–1000 m >1000 m	Not suitable Less suitable Suitable
	Distance to major roads	[86]	250–750 m 750–1000 m <250 m, >1000 m	Suitable Less suitable Not suitable
	Population density	[87]	<5000 m 5000–10000 m >10000 m	Suitable Less suitable Not suitable
	Slope	[85]	<10% 10–15% >15%	Suitable Less suitable Not suitable
	Distance to green spaces	[88]	<1000 m 1000–2000 m >2000 m	Suitable Less suitable Not suitable
	Distance to fire stations	[89,90]	<1000 m 1000–2000 m >2000 m	Suitable Less suitable Not suitable

- Slope,
    - It is suggested that the site of medical centres and hospitals be flat for an easy and low-cost construction [76].
- Distance from green spaces,
    - It is recommended that healthcare facilities are surrounded by natural environments to reduce air and noise pollution and the stress and pressure of patients [73].
- Distance from fire stations,
    - Fire stations should be placed in the proximity of public services such as hospitals because of the presence of a large number of people (staffs and patients) and the need for their safety [77].

The applied criteria for primary schools site selection were (Table 2.5):

- Slope/elevation,
    - The location of schools should be flat to have an easy and low-cost construction [65].

Table 2.5 Criteria of the land suitability analysis for primary schools

Land use	Criteria	Reference	Reclass	Level of suitability
Primary school	Slope	[91]	0–10 degree	Suitable
			10–20 degree	Less suitable
			>20 degree	Not suitable
	Elevation		<30 m	Suitable
			30–60 m	Less suitable
			>60 m	Not suitable
	Distance to commercial areas		>1000 m	Suitable
			500–1000 m	Less suitable
			0–500 m	Not suitable
	Distance to existing primary schools	[92]	>1500 m	Suitable
			1000–1500 m	Less suitable
			0–1000 m	Not suitable
	Distance to main road	[91]	>300 m	Suitable
			150–300 m	Less suitable
			<150 m	Not suitable
	Distance to residential areas	[93]	0–1000 m	Suitable
			1000–1500 m	Less suitable
			>1500 m	Not suitable

- Distance from commercial areas,

  - Due to the fact that commercial areas cause heavy traffic and pollution, schools should be reasonably located far from this type of land use [18].

- Proximity to residential areas,

  - Schools should be located in a walkable distance from residential areas. A 20-minute rule is often considered as a maximum travel time from residential regions to primary schools [78].

- Distance to main roads,

  - The location of new primary schools should be far from the major roads because of the safety of students and the negative impacts of traffic, air and noise pollution [65, 79].

- Distance to existing primary schools,

  - The location of new schools should not be in the proximity of existing primary schools [65].

As the next step, to develop the final suitability map, the pairwise comparison of the selected criteria was done through AHP to obtain the criteria weights. Table 2.6 presents the pairwise comparison matrix and obtained weights for primary schools, hospitals and green spaces criteria.

Finally, the suitability map for the required urban land uses were achieved through overlaying the reclassified maps and their obtained weights in AHP. Figure 2.7 depicts the final suitability map for primary schools, hospitals and green spaces.

According to the developed analysis, 11,712 hectares of the area were found suitable for the primary school whereas 292,566 and 16,827 hectares were identified less suitable and not suitable, respectively. In the similar vein and as to the final suitability map of green spaces, 148,717 hectares of the area were computed as the suitable region whereas around 186,000 hectares were identified not suitable for proposing new green spaces. The land use map of hospitals also indicates 117,897 hectares of the suitable area while more than 215,000 hectares belong to the less and not suitable ones for locating hospitals (Table 2.7).

Proposing the Areas

Accordingly, it was computed that 297,284, 41,493 and 315,011 hectares of residential regions of Beijing lack suitable access to primary schools, hospitals

Table 2.6 Pairwise comparison matrix and the criteria weights for primary schools, hospitals and green spaces

Criteria	Elevation	Slope	Distance from road	Distance from historical-cultural attractions	Distance from existing park	Distance from educational areas	Distance to residential areas	Distance from commercial areas
						Green space		
Elevation	1		9	1	5	3	9	5
Slope			9	1	5	9	9	5
Distance from road				9	5	7	3	5
Distance from historical-cultural attractions					3	5	9	5
Distance from existing park						1	9	5
Distance from educational areas							3	1
Distance to residential areas								5
Distance from commercial areas								

(*Continued*)

Table 2.6 (Continued)

	Weight of each criteria						
Elevation	Slope	Distance from road	Distance from historical-cultural attractions	Distance from existing park	Distance from educational areas	Distance to residential areas	Distance from commercial areas
0.024	0.21	0.382	0.023	0.066	0.090	0.279	0.114

Hospital

Criteria	Distance to existing hospitals	Distance to major roads	Population density	Slope	Distance to green spaces	Distance to fire stations
Distance to existing hospitals		5	5	9	5	9
Distance to major roads			5	9	7	7
Population density				5	3	3
Slope					3	3
Distance to green spaces						1
Distance to fire stations						

	Weight of each criteria					
Distance to existing hospitals	Distance to major road	Population density	Slope	Distance to green spaces	Distance to fire stations	Distance to residential areas
0.273	0.501	0.103	0.025	0.051	0.047	

Primary school

Criteria	Distance to main roads	Distance to existing primary schools	Distance to commercial areas	Elevation	Slope	Distance to residential areas
Distance to main road		3	7	2	3	7
Distance to existing primary schools			9	9	9	1
Distance to commercial areas				7	3	9
Elevation					1	9
Slope						1
Distance to residential areas						

(Continued)

Table 2.6 (Continued)

Distance to main road	Distance to existing primary schools	Distance to commercial areas	Elevation	Slope	Distance to residential areas
			Weight of each criteria		
0.108	0.347	0.023	0.062	0.045	0.415

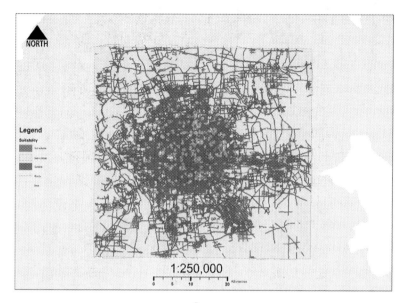

a

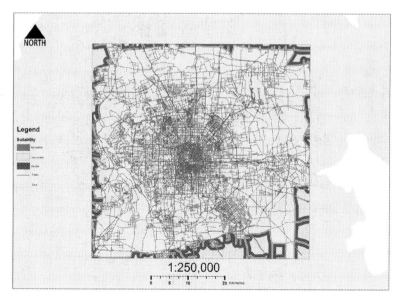

b

Figure 2.7 a) suitability map for green space. b) suitability map for hospital. c)
suitability map for primary school

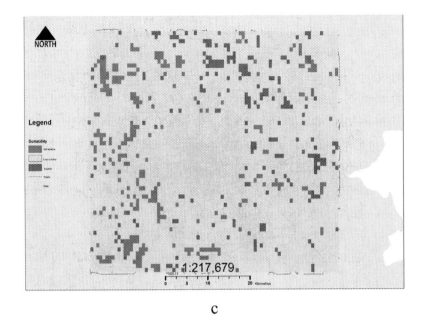

c

Figure 2.7 (Continued)

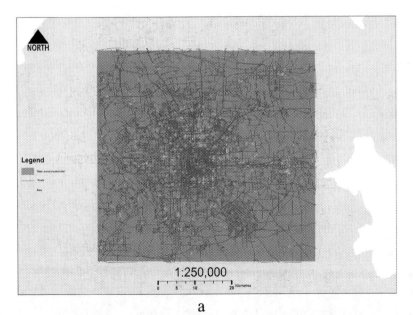

a

Figure 2.8 a) suitable areas proposed for green spaces. b) suitable areas proposed
for hospitals. c) suitable areas proposed for primary schools

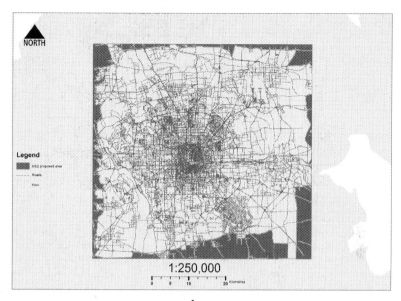

b

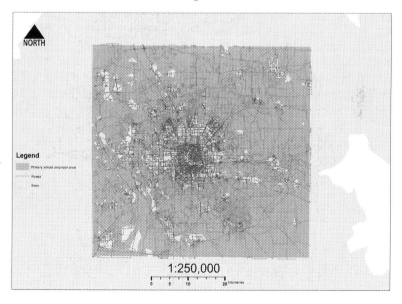

c

Figure 2.8 (Continued)

Table 2.7 Land suitability analysis and proposed areas

Land use	Suitable area (hec.)	Less suitable area (hec.)	Not suitable area (hec.)	Area without service	Proposed area
Green space	148717	172845	14.3	315011	306252
Hospital	117897	212865	2.7	41493	39140
Primary school	11712	292566	16827	297284	255823

and green spaces, respectively. Therefore, integrating the obtained final suitability maps for each land use and the maps specifying the regions which lack of each land use, suitable areas for locating the new land uses can now be proposed. Figure 2.8 illustrates the proposed areas for each land use. As a result, 255,823, 39,140 and 306,252 hectares were proposed for locating the new primary schools, healthcare facilities and green spaces, respectively (Table 2.7). Authorities can then apply these techniques and decide to locate these urban services with considering the ownership of ground and type (wasteland or not) and in line with the number of residents who need these services.

Conclusion

Balanced and optimized distribution of urban amenities (green spaces, primary schools, hospitals) was done based on the big data-driven site suitability analysis using social media data and Sina Weibo. Social media check-in points present the existing situation of urban services distribution of Beijing. It was perceived that urban services are mostly concentrated within the six-ring roads of Beijing and that the city has a monocentric spatial structure. In fact, most of the urban facilities are accumulated in one specific area which can lead to urban problems such as traffic, environmental pollution (air and noise) and social inequality. Thus, it is necessary to plan to distribute the urban services in numerous centres widely spread across Beijing instead of in one centre.

Furthermore, by analyzing the site suitability criteria of urban amenities, suitable sites were successfully determined for locating urban services. Residential regions of Beijing which are not within the proposed coverage of urban facilities are, therefore, proposed to have the priority of access to these facilities. Considering these criteria helps Beijing's residents have an equal access to urban services and enhance their quality of life. Moreover, social, environmental and economic sustainability can be further harmonized with a fair provision of the urban basic requirements for citizens.

Notes

1 Data were downloaded from www.beijingcitylab.com.
2 Data were downloaded from www.usgs.gov.

3 For further information, you can refer to T.L. Saaty. *The analytic hierarchy process: planning, priority setting, resources allocation.* New York: McGraw, 1980.

References

1 Hegazy, I.R. and M.R. Kaloop, Monitoring urban growth and land use change detection with GIS and remote sensing techniques in Daqahlia governorate Egypt. *International Journal of Sustainable Built Environment*, 2015. **4**(1): p. 117–124.

2 Zhang, L., et al., Evaluating urban land use efficiency with interacting criteria: An empirical study of cities in Jiangsu China. *Land Use Policy*, 2020. **90**: p. 104292.

3 Richardson, N., *Land use planning and sustainable development in Canada*. 1989.

4 Dambeebo, D. and C. Jallo, Sustainable urban development and land use management: Wa Municipality in perspective, Ghana. *Journal of Sustainable Development*, 2018. **11**(5): p. 235–248.

5 Dadhich, A.P., P.N. Dadhich, and R. Goyal, Multi temporal land-use land-cover change dynamics of Kota City, Rajasthan. *International Journal of Engineering and Advanced Technology*, 2017. **6**: p. 131–141.

6 He, C., et al., Evaluation of sustainable land management in urban area: A case study of Shanghai, China. *Ecological Indicators*, 2017. **80**: p. 106–113.

7 Khademi, S., M. Norouzi, and M. Hashemi, Sustainable land use evaluation based on preservative approach. *International Archives of the Photogrammetry, Remote Sensing & Spatial Information Sciences*, 2019.

8 Hassan, M.M. and M.N.I. Nazem, Examination of land use/land cover changes, urban growth dynamics, and environmental sustainability in Chittagong city, Bangladesh. *Environment, Development and Sustainability*, 2016. **18**(3): p. 697–716.

9 Deka, J., et al., Study on land-use and land-cover change dynamics in Eastern Arunachal Pradesh, NE India using remote sensing and GIS. *Tropical Ecology*, 2019. **60**(2): p. 199–208.

10 Owusu, S. and K. Asamoah, Servicing land for housing development in peri-urban areas of Kumasi, Ghana: Theory versus practice. *Journal of Science and Technology (Ghana)*, 2005. **25**(1): p. 77–85.

11 Enoguanbhor, E.C., et al., Land cover change in the Abuja City-Region, Nigeria: Integrating GIS and remotely sensed data to support land use planning. *Sustainability*, 2019. **11**(5): p. 1313.

12 Li, Y. and G. Liu, Characterizing spatiotemporal pattern of land use change and its driving force based on GIS and landscape analysis techniques in Tianjin during 2000–2015. *Sustainability*, 2017. **9**(6): p. 894.

13 Frias-Martinez, V. and E. Frias-Martinez, Spectral clustering for sensing urban land use using Twitter activity. *Engineering Applications of Artificial Intelligence*, 2014. **35**: p. 237–245.

14 Mangi, M.Y., et al., Urban land use planning trend and sustainable challenges in socio-economic development. *Mehran University Research Journal of Engineering and Technology*, 2018. **37**(2): p. 397–404.

15 Salehi, E. and S.H. Zahiri, Green space suitability analysis using evolutionary algorithm and weighted linear combination (WLC) method. *Space Ontology International Journal*, 2016. **5**(4): p. 51–60.

16 Liu, R., et al., Land-use suitability analysis for urban development in Beijing. *Journal of Environmental Management*, 2014. **145**: p. 170–179.

17 Huang, H., Q. Li, and Y. Zhang, Urban residential land suitability analysis combining remote sensing and social sensing data: A case study in Beijing, China. *Sustainability*, 2019. **11**(8): p. 2255.

18 Bukhari, Z., A. Rodzi, and A. Noordin, Spatial multi-criteria decision analysis for safe school site selection. *International Geoinformatics Research and Development Journal*, 2010. **1**(2): p. 1–14.

19 Wu, H., et al., Evaluation and planning of urban green space distribution based on mobile phone data and two-step floating catchment area method. *Sustainability*, 2018. **10**(1): p. 214.

20 Herold, M., X. Liu, and K.C. Clarke, Spatial metrics and image texture for mapping urban land use. *Photogrammetric Engineering & Remote Sensing*, 2003. **69**(9): p. 991–1001.

21 Pan, G., et al., Land-use classification using taxi GPS traces. *IEEE Transactions on Intelligent Transportation Systems*, 2012. **14**(1): p. 113–123.

22 Frias-Martinez, V., et al., *Sensing urban land use with Twitter activity*. Telefonica Research, Madrid, Spain, 2013.

23 Zhan, X., S.V. Ukkusuri, and F. Zhu, Inferring urban land use using large-scale social media check-in data. *Networks and Spatial Economics*, 2014. **14**(3–4): p. 647–667.

24 Soliman, A., et al., Social sensing of urban land use based on analysis of Twitter users' mobility patterns. *PloS One*, 2017. **12**(7): p. e0181657.

25 Xu, H., Application of GPS-RTK technology in the land change survey. *Procedia Engineering*, 2012. **29**: p. 3454–3459.

26 Wu, S.-S., et al., Using geometrical, textural, and contextual information of land parcels for classification of detailed urban land use. *Annals of the Association of American Geographers*, 2009. **99**(1): p. 76–98.

27 Malarvizhi, K., S.V. Kumar, and P. Porchelvan, Use of high resolution Google Earth satellite imagery in landuse map preparation for urban related applications. *Procedia Technology*, 2016. **24**: p. 1835–1842.

28 Rawat, J. and M. Kumar, Monitoring land use/cover change using remote sensing and GIS techniques: A case study of Hawalbagh block, district Almora, Uttarakhand, India. *The Egyptian Journal of Remote Sensing and Space Science*, 2015. **18**(1): p. 77–84.

29 Barakat, A., et al., Land use/land cover change and environmental impact assessment in Béni-Mellal district (Morocco) using remote sensing and GIS. *Earth Systems and Environment*, 2019. **3**(1): p. 113–125.

30 Pei, T., et al., A new insight into land use classification based on aggregated mobile phone data. *International Journal of Geographical Information Science*, 2014. **28**(9): p. 1988–2007.

31 Liu, X., et al., Classifying urban land use by integrating remote sensing and social media data. *International Journal of Geographical Information Science*, 2017. **31**(8): p. 1675–1696.

32 Hu, T., et al., Mapping urban land use by using Landsat images and open social data. *Remote Sensing*, 2016. **8**(2): p. 151.

33 Mao, H., G. Thakur, and B. Bhaduri. Exploiting mobile phone data for multi-category land use classification in Africa. In *Proceedings of the 2nd ACM SIG-SPATIAL Workshop on Smart Cities and Urban Analytics*. 2016.

34 Xing, J. and R.E. Sieber, A land use/land cover change geospatial cyberinfrastructure to integrate big data and temporal topology. *International Journal of Geographical Information Science*, 2016. **30**(3): p. 573–593.

35 Temiz, F., A. Bozdag, and S.S. Durduran, Analysis of land-use change in Denizli City Center through geographical information systems. *Fresenius Environmental Bulletin*, 2018. **27**(9): p. 6129–6136.

36 Toole, J.L., et al. Inferring land use from mobile phone activity. In *Proceedings of the ACM SIGKDD International Workshop on Urban Computing*. 2012. ACM.

37 Lian, J. and L. Zhang. One-month Beijing taxi GPS trajectory dataset with taxi IDs and vehicle status. In *Proceedings of the First Workshop on Data Acquisition to Analysis*. 2018.

38 Zhang, K., et al., Analyzing spatiotemporal congestion pattern on urban roads based on taxi GPS data. *Journal of Transport and Land Use*, 2017. **10**(1): p. 675–694.

39 Mazimpaka, J.D. and S. Timpf, Exploring the potential of combining taxi GPS and Flickr data for discovering functional regions. In *AGILE 2015*. 2015, Springer. p. 3–18.

40 Yuan, J., Y. Zheng, and X. Xie. Discovering regions of different functions in a city using human mobility and POIs. In *Proceedings of the 18th ACM SIGKDD International Conference on Knowledge Discovery and Data Mining*. 2012.

41 Liu, X., et al., Identification of urban functional regions in Chengdu based on Taxi Trajectory Time series data. *ISPRS International Journal of Geo-Information*, 2020. **9**(3): p. 158.

42 Qi, G., et al. Measuring social functions of city regions from large-scale taxi behaviors. In *2011 IEEE International Conference on Pervasive Computing and Communications Workshops (PERCOM Workshops)*. 2011. IEEE.

43 Liu, Y., et al., Urban land uses and traffic 'source-sink areas': Evidence from GPS-enabled taxi data in Shanghai. *Landscape and Urban Planning*, 2012. **106**(1): p. 73–87.

44 WANG, Y.-q., et al., Urban area division and function discovery based on trajectory data. *DEStech Transactions on Computer Science and Engineering*, 2017(aita).

45 Fan, K., et al. Discovering urban social functional regions using taxi trajectories. In *2015 IEEE 12th International Conference on Ubiquitous Intelligence and Computing and 2015 IEEE 12th International Conference on Autonomic and Trusted Computing and 2015 IEEE 15th International Conference on Scalable Computing and Communications and Its Associated Workshops (UIC-ATC-ScalCom)*. 2015. IEEE.

46 Akhmad Nuzir, F. and B. Julien Dewancker, Dynamic land-use map based on Twitter data. *Sustainability*, 2017. **9**(12): p. 2158.

47 Wang, Y., et al., Mapping dynamic urban land use patterns with crowdsourced geo-tagged social media (Sina-Weibo) and commercial points of interest collections in Beijing, China. *Sustainability*, 2016. **8**(11): p. 1202.

48 Zhang, X., et al., A new approach to refining land use types: Predicting point-of-interest categories using Weibo Check-in data. *ISPRS International Journal of Geo-Information*, 2020. **9**(2): p. 124.

49 Preoţiuc-Pietro, D. and T. Cohn. Mining user behaviours: A study of check-in patterns in location based social networks. In *Proceedings of the 5th Annual ACM Web Science Conference*. 2013.

50 Tu, W., et al., Coupling mobile phone and social media data: A new approach to understanding urban functions and diurnal patterns. *International Journal of Geographical Information Science*, 2017. **31**(12): p. 2331–2358.

51 Cao, J., et al. Exploring the distribution and dynamics of functional regions using mobile phone data and social media data. In *Proceedings of the 14th International Conference on Computers in Urban Planning and Urban Management, Boston, MA, USA*. 2015.

52 Aung, T., K.K. Lwin, and Y. Sekimoto, Identification and classification of land use types in Yangon City by using mobile Call Detail Records (CDRs) data. *Journal of the Eastern Asia Society for Transportation Studies*, 2019. **13**: p. 1114–1133.

53 Soto, V. and E. Frías-Martínez. Automated land use identification using cell-phone records. In *Proceedings of the 3rd ACM international Workshop on MobiArch*. 2011.

54 Soto, V. and E. Frías-Martínez. Robust land use characterization of urban landscapes using cell phone data. In *Proceedings of the 1st Workshop on Pervasive Urban Applications, in Conjunction with 9th International Conference Pervasive Computing*. 2011.

55 Yuan, G., et al., Recognition of functional areas based on Call Detail Records and Point of Interest data. *Journal of Advanced Transportation*, 2020. **2020**.

56 WorldAtlas. *The world's most populated capital cities*. 2018 [cited 2020 30/06]; Available from: www.worldatlas.com/articles/the-world-s-most-populated-capital-cities.html.

57 Yang, Y., et al., Quantifying spatio-temporal patterns of urban expansion in Beijing during 1985–2013 with rural-urban development transformation. *Land Use Policy*, 2018. **74**: p. 220–230.

58 Liu, Y., et al., Spatial pattern of leisure activities among residents in Beijing, China: Exploring the impacts of urban environment. *Sustainable Cities and Society*, 2020. **52**: p. 101806.

59 Xu, Q., X. Zheng, and M. Zheng, Do urban planning policies meet sustainable urbanization goals? A scenario-based study in Beijing, China. *Science of the Total Environment*, 2019. **670**: p. 498–507.

60 Sun, C., et al., Urban land development for industrial and commercial use: A case study of Beijing. *Sustainability*, 2016. **8**(12): p. 1323.

61 Moussa, M. and A.J.P.E.S. Abou Elwafa, *School site selection process*, 2017. **37**: p. 282–293.

62 Ustaoglu, E., A.J.U.F. Aydınoglu, and U. Greening, Site suitability analysis for green space development of Pendik district (Turkey). *Urban Forestry & Urban Greening*, 2020. **47**: p. 126542.

63 Li, F., et al., Spatiotemporal patterns of the use of urban green spaces and external factors contributing to their use in central Beijing. *International Journal of Environmental Research and Public Health*, 2017. **14**(3): p. 237.

64 Adalı, E.A. and A. Tuş, Hospital site selection with distance-based multi-criteria decision-making methods. *International Journal of Healthcare Management*, 2019: p. 1–11.

65 Ali, K.A., Multi-criteria decision analysis for primary school site selection in Al-Mahaweel district using GIS technique. *Journal of Kerbala University*, 2018. **16**(1): p. 342–350.

66 Abebe, M.T. and T.L. Megento, Urban green space development using GIS-based multi-criteria analysis in Addis Ababa metropolis. *Applied Geomatics*, 2017. **9**(4): p. 247–261.

67 Pareta, K. and U. Pareta, *GIS based multi-criteria analysis for urban green space development: A case study of Daltonganj Town, Jharkhand*, 2019. **5**(2): p. 40–48.

68 Rehnuma, M., M.J.M. Yusof, and S.A. Bakar, *Emerging green spaces in north of Dhaka: Suitability analysis in a dense urban settlement*, 2007.

69 Pokhrel, S., Green space suitability evaluation for urban resilience: An analysis of Kathmandu Metropolitan city, Nepal. *Environmental Research Communications*, 2019. **1**(10): p. 105003.

70 Ustaoglu, E. and A.C. Aydınoglu, Land suitability assessment of green infrastructure development. *TeMA-Journal of Land Use, Mobility and Environment*, 2019. **12**(2): p. 165–178.

71 Teimouri, R. and L.S. Vand, GIS techniques for suitable locations for urban green space in district 2 of Tabriz, City, Iran. *Ambient Science*, 2017. **4**(2).

72 Agus, F., et al., The geographic information system development for selection of green open space in urban densely area. *Jurnal Infotel*, 2018. **10**(3): p. 125–130.

73 Oppio, A., et al., Addressing decisions about new hospitals' siting: A multidimensional evaluation approach. *Annali dell'Istituto Superiore di Sanità*, 2016. **52**(1): p. 78–87.

74 Soltani, A. and E.Z. Marandi, Hospital site selection using two-stage fuzzy multi-criteria decision making process. *Journal of Urban and Environmental Engineering*, 2011. **5**(1): p. 32–43.

75 Abdullahi, S., A.R.b. Mahmud, and B. Pradhan, Spatial modelling of site suitability assessment for hospitals using geographical information system-based multicriteria approach at Qazvin city, Iran. *Geocarto International*, 2014. **29**(2): p. 164–184.

76 Nsaif, Q.A., S.M. Khaleel, and A.H. Khateeb, Integration of GIS and remote sensing technique for hospital site selection in Baquba district. *Journal of Engineering Science and Technology*, 2020. **15**(3): p. 1492–1505.

77 Parsa Moghadam, M., et al., Optimal site selection of urban hospitals using GIS software in Ardabil City. *Journal of Ardabil University of Medical Sciences*, 2017. **16**(4): p. 374–388.

78 Moussa, M. and A. Abou Elwafa, School site selection process. *Procedia Environmental Sciences*, 2017. **37**: p. 282–293.

79 Samad, A.M., et al. A study on school location suitability using AHP in GIS approach. In *2012 IEEE 8th International Colloquium on Signal Processing and Its Applications. 2012*. IEEE.

80 Mahmoud, A. H. A. and M. A. El-Sayed, Development of sustainable urban green areas in Egyptian new cities: The case of El-Sadat City. *Landscape and Urban Planning*, 2011. **101**(2): p. 157–170.

81 Teimouri, R. and L. S. Vand, GIS techniques for suitable locations for urban green space in district 2 of Tabriz, City, Iran. *Ambient Science*, 2017. **4**(2).

82 Abebe, M. T. and T. L. Megento, Urban green space development using GIS-based multi-criteria analysis in Addis Ababa metropolis. *Applied Geomatics*, 2017. **9**(4): p. 247–261.

83 Pokhrel, S., Green space suitability evaluation for urban resilience: An analysis of Kathmandu Metropolitan city, Nepal. *Environmental Research Communications*, 2019. **1**(10): p. 105003.

84 Ustaoglu, E. and A. C. Aydınoglu, Land suitability assessment of green infrastructure development. *TeMA-Journal of Land Use, Mobility and Environment*, 2019. **12**(2): p. 165–178.

85 Nsaif, Q.A., S.M. Khaleel, and A.H. Khateeb, Integration of GIS and remote sensing technique for hospital site selection in Baquba district. *Journal of Engineering Science and Technology*, 2020. **15**(3): p. 1492–1505.

86 Halder, B., et al., Assessment of hospital sites' suitability by spatial information technologies using AHP and GIS-based multi-criteria approach of Rajpur–Sonarpur Municipality. *Modeling Earth Systems and Environment*, 2020: p. 1–16.

87 Parvin F, Ali SA, Hashmi S, and A. Khatoon. Accessibility and site suitability for healthcare services using GIS-based hybrid decision-making approach: a study in Murshidabad, India. *Spatial Information Research*, 2021. **29**(1): p. 1–18.

88 Soltani, A. and E. Z. Marandi, Hospital site selection using two-stage fuzzy multi-criteria decision making process. *Journal of Urban and Environmental Engineering*, 2011. **5**(1): p. 32–43.

89 Abdullahi, S., A.R.b. Mahmud, and B. Pradhan, Spatial modelling of site suitability assessment for hospitals using geographical information system-based multicriteria approach at Qazvin city, Iran. *Geocarto International*, 2014. **29**(2): p. 164–184.

90 Parsa Moghadam, M., et al., Optimal site selection of urban hospitals using GIS software in Ardabil City. *Journal of Ardabil University of Medical Sciences*, 2017. **16**(4): p. 374–388.

91 Bukhari, Z., A. Rodzi, and A. Noordin, Spatial multi-criteria decision analysis for safe school site selection. *International Geoinformatics Research and Development Journal*, 2010. **1**(2): p. 1–14.

92 Jamal, I., Multi-criteria GIS analysis for school site selection in Gorno-Badakhshan autonomous Oblast, Tajikistan. *Master Thesis in Geographical Information Science*, 2016.

93 Moussa, M. and A. Abou Elwafa, School site selection process. *Procedia Environmental Sciences*, 2017. **37**: p. 282–293.

3 Big Data in Urban Traffic and Transportation

Traffic and Transportation Structure in Urban Planning

The pulse of a city is created through human movement [1] as it allows people to participate in urban activities [2]. Transportation networks are, hence, an essential component of the daily life in developing and developed societies for providing mobility to all travellers [3]. It becomes a substantial base for the economic growth [4] and plays a fundamental role in urban development planning [5]. In line with this trend, however, the rapid growth of population and urban development causes struggle in the transportation systems in cities since it cannot be balanced with the ever-increasing demand for urban mobility [6]. This issue results in critical traffic congestion, and increasing travel time, fuel consumption and air pollution in many large cities around the world [3].

Analyzing the mechanisms and identifying the attributes of human movement are necessary for sustainable transportation and urban planning [7]. This implies the necessity of rethinking the transportation planning to cope better with the demand in the future. In fact, transportation planning is a complicated process including a precise prediction of future requirements and investigation of current travel patterns in cities [8]. The primary purpose here is to match the transportation supply with travel demand, which indicates 'requirement'. Hence, a complete perception of this requirement is necessary for identifying and analyzing traffic-related problems [9]. This task, if performed properly, can provide mobility in a safe, efficient and economical manner to support economic growth and sustainable transport development [10], one of the primary concepts of sustainable urban mobility. This virtue can be conducted socially comprehensively and environmentally sustainably as a result of a set of transport guidelines and movements to provide broad and equal access to urban areas, to prioritize non-motorized and public transport modes and to avoid spatial segregation [11]. This could lay a basis for the general urban structure development and transport improvement, especially for the public transport system expansion [12].

DOI: 10.4324/9781003139942-3

All in all, urban engineers require developed data to design, plan and manage transportation networks in the sustainable approach. These datasets should reflect mobility patterns, recognition of home-work locations and commuting routes through the smart and environmentally friendly technical solutions [13]. By getting access to advanced and emerging big data technologies, a variety of spatiotemporal data is produced and used in analyzing the current situation of cities in real time, followed by the application in transportation planning [3].

Smart Traffic Control and Monitoring Through Big Data

Background

With the unprecedented growth of urbanization, traffic congestion becomes a critical issue all over the world because the application of existing transport systems overpasses its current capacity [14]. This issue negatively impacts sustainability and liveability in big cities [14] because traffic congestion influences on urban road networks and diminishes travel performance [15]. For instance, Tehran with more than 14 million people suffers from severe traffic congestion in the rush hours. As a result, it is important to measure the traffic network situation to eliminate the issues related to congestion, safety, air quality [16], energy consumption and the decay of the urban ecological environment [14]. It is argued that, if the locations and time of traffic congestion are precisely recognized, authorities and transport managers can take appropriate strategies based on the obtained patterns for alleviating the traffic congestion [17].

Big data sources provide opportunities to collect real-time traffic data including spatial and temporal information. This low-cost process is performed through the contribution of a large number of people using mobile devices and smartphones [18]. In this section, the application of social media data and GPS trajectories is explained for traffic monitoring and identification of traffic congestion.

GPS Trajectories for Traffic Monitoring and Congestion Detection

GPS trajectories data are considered as a promising big data source for traffic monitoring in real time [19] in light of the extensive deployment of GPS devices. It is an alternative method to surveillance and can discover the traffic operation performance in extensive traffic networks [15, 17]. It is stated that analyzing both of the spatial and temporal patterns of the traffic situation is feasible through GPS data [15].

Applying GPS trajectories for traffic patterns detection and estimation has a clear step-by-step process. First, GPS real-time traces, which constitute a sequence of GPS points [20] and have features including recording time, position information coordinates (longitude, latitude) and vehicle velocity [21, 22], are extracted during the specified time interval and in designated periods from smartphones equipped with GPS sensors, taxi GPS trajectories and/or GPS trackers [20]. Second, the obtained GPS traces are pre-processed [20] and the road segments which do not have adequate data are eliminated [23]. Following that, through map matching methods, trip data points are transferred to maps. In other word, coordinates of vehicles are linked with digital maps (open street map road networks [24]) in order to place the position of vehicles in underlying road segments [21, 25]. Hence, precise map matchings can be obtained via identifying the travel directions and distances to the closest roads and discovering the related segments [19, 20]. In the next step, the average speed of vehicles are estimated on every road segment [19, 25]. The traffic condition is, then, estimated and assessed based on the vehicle speed performance index because this is one of the indicative factors for traffic congestion [21]. The congestion index is calculated through the speed-based congestion measure [24] and changes in the range from 0 to 100. The value of 100 shows the most congested condition and the value near to 0 presents a free-flow condition [21]. Then, clustering algorithms and machine learning methods such as Fuzzy-C means clustering and Density-Based Spatial Clustering (DBSCN) are applied to classify the road segments based on their speed patterns [21, 26].

In this technique, the score of the traffic pattern is mapped and fuzzified according to real traffic situations and GIS visualization in various levels such as free flow, light traffic, heavy traffic, stationary traffic [27] or incident, slowed traffic, very slowed and blocked traffic [21]. Finally, the information related to the traffic condition is reported through a traveller information system [27].

Some advantages can enumerate to using GPS technology for traffic monitoring:

- It is a cost-effective tool, available on smartphones and provides a real-time traffic assessment [19],
- This technology can cover an extensive area of road networks for traffic monitoring [19, 28],
- Data obtained by this tool have a high quality for traffic monitoring [17],
- Drivers can decrease their travel time and travel delay by obtaining the knowledge from this technology [17]. Passengers can alter their routes to avoid getting stuck in traffic jams while dynamically providing accurate and reliable route information [20],
- Temporal coverage can be extended for traffic monitoring [28],

- Trajectories data can be obtained without laborious work [28],
- It overcomes the installation and maintenance costs of traditional monitoring systems [20],
- This technology can be conveniently used for roads which do not have monitoring systems [20].

However, applying this technology has some challenges, for instance:

- Finding and applying efficient estimation algorithms is a challenge in using GPS-technology for traffic evaluation [19],
- External factors such as weather and road conditions influence the data accuracy [19],
- GPS technology may encounter some software or hardware bugs during the data collection procedure [17],
- Tall buildings in urban areas act as an obstacle for GPS signals in the traffic monitoring process [28],
- GPS applications may need some privacy and permission protocols [20],
- It is not feasible to gather GPS traces in too-short time intervals through smartphones because it quickly drains the battery [20]. Moreover, with large intervals, it is difficult to determine a real trajectory for traffic monitoring [29],
- Transferring the GPS coordinates from a small number of vehicles in road networks can lead to a delay in discovering congestion [20],
- Locating the vehicles on the map is also a challenge in using GPS traces [20].

It can be concluded that, despite the challenges of GPS technology for traffic monitoring, it is a handy tool for city authorities and traffic managers to identify the traffic obstacles and control urban mobility. This tool can effectively complement traditional traffic sensors such as loop detectors and cameras [20].

Social Media Data for Traffic Monitoring

Traffic is one of the issues which people talk about in their daily life. They tend to share traffic-related information via social media networks such as Twitter, Facebook and WhatsApp when there is an accident, car crash, roadwork or road closure. For instance, the traffic situation of Istanbul, the capital city of Turkey, is reported through traffic Tweets and its real-time intensity map is available online[1] and can be observed through mobile apps. These types of networks are user-generated content which presents precious traffic information for researchers and authorities to develop predictive insights towards traffic monitoring [18].

This technique provides data features such as timestamps, geo-location (longitude and latitude coordinates) and text contents, and its application has a process with specified steps [18]. The first step is to pre-process the geo social media data based on the identified keywords [18] and during the specified time for a specific urban area. The pre-processing stage is carried out through natural language processing techniques. It contains actions for eliminating the repeated posts [30], tokenization and word cutting, removing stop words (articles, conjunctions, prepositions, pronouns [31]), correcting spelling errors, slang replacement, stemming (diminishing and reducing each word to its stem or root form [32]), feature representation [33], discarding all web URLs, special characters and punctuation marks [34].

The pre-processed data are then classified through either manual labelling (which is a time-consuming process) or machine learning classifiers such as Support Vector Machine, Naïve Bayes and Decision Tree to classify the social media data and distinguish traffic events [30] from non-traffic ones [34]. Following the classification, traffic-related ones are further classified into the exact events such as traffic accidents, road closures, roadworks and special events [18] through structural labelling methods such as the Supervised Latent Dirichlet Allocation algorithm [34].

In the next step, an accurate location of traffic events should be identified. The geo-coding procedure can be done here through extracting location information from user profiles, the GPS coordinates which are tagged to social media data and/or content of posts. Finally, the traffic events locations are visualized in a map on smartphones or web-based applications [18] to recognize the traffic density on roads [30], or to transfer data to traffic management centres [34].

The results can be validated through various methods like direct communication with the people who were present in the event, reports drawn up by the police and/or local administrations (available only in case of incidents), road condition reports and incident data systems [35], radio traffic news, official real-time traffic news websites and local newspapers [32].

Applying geo-tagged social media data for monitoring traffic has some advantages including:

• Social media data provide semantic information about the reasons for traffic conditions and drivers can plan for their routes through the reported traffic events [18] and choose the shortest and fastest driving routes [34],
• Social media data provide the real-time traffic situation in a low-cost manner [35, 36],

- Human behaviours and feelings about transportation systems and traffic events can be surveyed [36],
- These datasets can be accessed easily to collect rich information about traffic situations [37],
- Social media data as the ubiquitous data source can cover remarkably extensive areas for traffic monitoring [34, 35],
- Traffic conditions can be announced through platforms like Twitter sooner than other websites and local newspapers [32, 34],
- This can be used for the regions (urban and suburban) which do not have traffic sensors [32],
- External reasons for traffic such as football matches, processions and demonstrations can be identified [32].

On the other hand, utilizing social media for traffic congestion monitoring faces some challenges:

- Social media data can contain irregular, non-standardized and vague tones [35], informal and abbreviated words, a large number of spelling and grammatical mistakes, inappropriate sentence structures, mixed languages, meaningless messages, and rumours which may make it less reliable [18, 32],
- The location deviation may occur because a user may post a message about a traffic situation in a different location than the original event occurs [18],
- This type of data collection and analysis may be totally hindered if internet reception gets obscured [30],
- The recognition of intensity, sarcasm, emotions and feelings is difficult through words [30].

Holistically, the geo-tagged social media data is a cost-effective and functional method for traffic information collection [34, 35], which provides daily patterns and peak hours of traffic incidents and leads to enhancing the operation of traffic management centres.

Summary

It can be concluded that the presented big data technologies including social media and GPS trajectories can practically complement the existing sources of real-time traffic monitoring. During the processing of social media data for traffic monitoring, the types and reasons behind the traffic congestion are visualized and the location and intensity are developed using GPS trajectories and speed patterns. Figure 3.1 indicates the process of using social media data and GPS trajectories for discovering the traffic patterns.

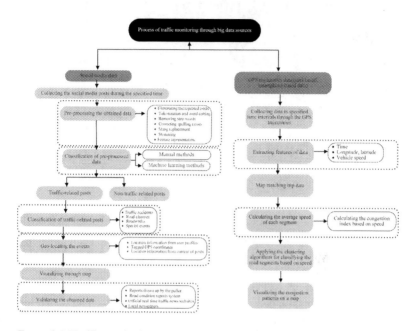

Figure 3.1 Traffic monitoring process through big data technologies

Table 3.1 Tools for big data collection in traffic monitoring

Tools	GPS trajectories	Geo-tagged social media data
Type of data	• Spatial and temporal	• Spatial and temporal • Descriptive
Features extracted	• Time • Location (latitude, longitude) • Speed of vehicles	• Time and location of posts • Number of posts • Texts and contents of posts
Methodology for processing data	• Classifying the traffic intensity of road segments based on average speed	• Classifying traffic-related posts and geo-locating them

In terms of the data delivery, social media provide semantic information on top of spatial and temporal data while GPS trajectories deliver information about the severity and intensity of traffic congestion (Table 3.1). Therefore, both incidents and patterns of traffic congestions can be identified by analyzing the obtained data. All in all, both technologies can support each other for a proper surveillance of traffic situations.

Big Data Application in Transportation Behaviour and Patterns

Background

Figuring out the travel behaviour demand assists with developing proper urban transportation and sustainable regenerative planning for cities [38]. In fact, two-thirds of the global energy use in cities are consumed due to the transportation of residents commuting [39]. With this respect, big data applications are applied to identify residents' travel behaviours, which are influenced by factors such as the spatial structure of a city, land uses and urban road networks [7]. Analyzing travel behaviour consists of identifying trip purposes, departure time, travel durations, travel distances, trip sequences, trip destinations, daily trip frequencies and complex trip chains [40].

Therefore, it is necessary to identify the dynamics of the residents' daily and hidden mobility patterns and anomalies for the planning and management of urban facilities, services and traffic prediction [1]. However, it is difficult to use traditional methods such as questionnaires, observations and surveys to precisely and profoundly investigate human mobility [41] as these techniques are expensive and outdated [40]. Hence, in the next section, the applications of SCD and taxi GPS trajectories are explained for the transportation behaviour analysis [42].

Smart Card Data for Transportation Behaviour

Electronic payments in public transport using SCD provide precious and enormous spatial and temporal data to effectively investigate travel behaviour [43, 44]. Through this technique, spatial data indicates the places which commuters regularly visit on multiple days and temporal data shows the same time periods in which travellers begin and finish their daily trips [44, 45].

Travel behaviour patterns from SCD can be extracted based on the following process. First, smart card IDs, travel time (boarding time, alight time), locations of the origin and destination (boarding and alighting stops) and route IDs are elicited for each trip. The records which have faulty transaction times are removed during the pre-processing stage. Trips are then identified from continuous tap-in and tap-out transactions. In other words, trip chain (a series of trips made by travellers on a daily basis) information is constructed for each passenger. A trip, in this context, means a movement from the location of an origin to the location of a destination where an activity such as commuting between home to work is done [46].

Two main principles can be considered to deduce trips from individual transactions. Firstly, the time interval between transactions must be less than

60 minutes. Secondly, the origin stop of the first transaction must be distinct from the destination stop of the second one [47]. Some features such as number of travel days, number of similar first boarding times, number of similar route sequences and the number of similar stop ID sequences are extracted from trip chains for clustering. The most frequent travel patterns are then recognized based on DBSCAN algorithms. Following that, clustering algorithms such as k-means can be used for categorizing the travel pattern regularities [42, 45, 47]. The regularities should be measured via temporal and spatial patterns. Temporal patterns are calculated through the similarity of travel and departure time and the number of traveling days and spatial patterns can be indicated by route-level, origin and destinations similarities [47, 48].

Based on the obtained regularities, passengers with regular travel times, passengers with regular origin-destinations, passengers without regular travel times and origin-destinations and passengers without any regularity are identified [47], and morning and evening peak hours are specified [1, 43].

Utilizing SCD for the analysis of travel behaviour and patterns benefits from the following advantages:

- Based on the features such as the start time and duration of an activity, the type of travel behaviour and temporal and spatial patterns, primary activity types (home, work, leisure activities) can be effectively inferred [42, 43, 46],
- This method is functional for evaluating, enhancing and optimizing public transportation services and finding the factors which allure customers of public transportation [45],
- This is an efficient and convenient data source for extracting the short-term and long-term travel patterns of residents [43, 45, 48].

On the other hand, the challenges are:

- On some occasions, some features of data are renamed because of privacy. This fact necessitates using effective data mining methods to deduce the travel behaviour patterns [45],
- Available computer technologies have physical memory limitations for processing and clustering a massive amount of SCD [45],
- Travel trip identification from individual transactions of passengers and creating a consistency among the trip chains are substantial for identifying travel patterns [43, 47].

At the end of this section, it can be mentioned that novel aspects of mobility patterns and the correlation between human mobility and land uses can be identified by SCD within time and space [1].

Taxi GPS Trajectories for Transportation Behaviour

Generally speaking, taxis are one of the popular travel modes for residents reflecting residents' travel behaviour [49]. Taxi GPS trajectory data can be a precious source to find out passengers' demand and drivers' operation behaviour [50]. As mentioned previously, taxi GPS trajectory data is defined as a sequence of a taxi's continuous geo-referenced coordinates, and its timestamps encompass a large amount of temporal and spatial information of urban residents' activity patterns [51]. The features extracted from taxi trajectories data for travel behaviour analysis are trip information including time, pick-up and drop-off locations (latitude and longitude), origin and destination of complete trips, speed and direction of vehicles, operation status (occupied, vacant or stopped) and trip distances [52].

There is a clear process for identifying the travel behaviour from taxi GPS trajectories. First of all, GPS traces should be pre-processed and anomalies like records without location information (latitude or longitude) or outside of the study area should be removed [49]. Likewise, unreliable points should be discarded [41] and very small trips and/or long trips should be excluded from the analysis [50, 53]. Then, the number of pick-up and drop-off points for equal interval time (e.g., one hour) are counted. The spatial and temporal distribution of taxi travels and their similarities are analyzed through spatial clustering algorithms such as DBSCAN or grid density-based algorithms [7, 51]. Following that, the hotspot areas for travel demands and hot paths between attractive areas in various time periods are recognized in urban areas [51]. During this process, the temporal pattern distributions (peak hours) and spatial pattern distributions (pick-up and drop-off points) during weekdays and weekends are identified [49]. Ultimately, spatial and temporal distributions can be visualized through OD matrixes (Figure 3.2), chord diagram plots (Figure 3.3) [41] or GIS maps.

Advantages which can be enumerated for using taxi trajectories for travel behaviour analysis are:

- GPS taxi trajectories data have a great geographical resolution and can cover travel trajectories in the scale of a city and in a wide distribution [49, 51],
- This type of dataset has a high precision and cohesion and a high level of automation [41],
- A precise analysis of travel behaviour through this technique presents powerful methods to amend the quality of public transport services [41],

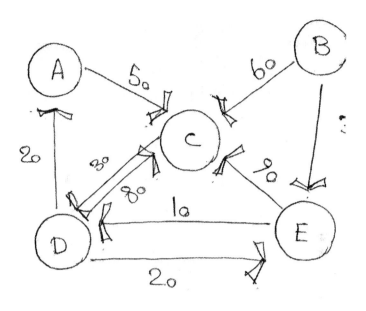

	A	B	C	D	E	T
A	o	o	5o	o	o	5o
B	o	o	6o	o	3o	9o
C	o	o	o	3o	o	3o
D	2o	o	8o	o	2o	12o
E	o	o	9o	1o	o	1oo
T	2o	o	28o	4o	5o	39o

Figure 3.2 OD matrix sample

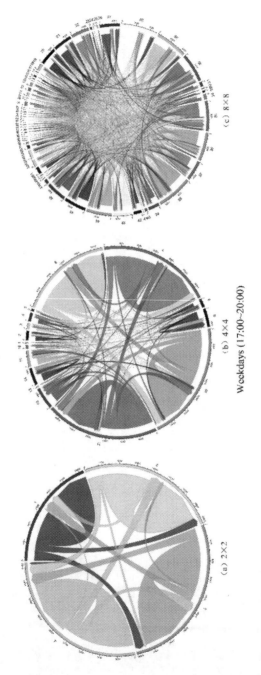

Figure 3.3 Chord diagram sample of OD flow

- Origin and destination from GPS taxi trajectories have a greater precision in analyzing urban mobility, compared with other public transportations [53],
- Urban land use and structure of a city can be indicated by taxi trip patterns [54].

However, some challenges can be considered for using taxi GPS trajectories in travel behaviour:

- It is a hard task to use taxi GPS data for a travel survey, because taxis do not have fixed paths [49],
- The blockage of buildings and GPS equipment destruction leads to redundancy and data loss of taxi GPS trajectories [49],
- Taxi trajectories have some difficulties such as noise, redundancy of data, missing values, inconsistencies and incomplete data [51].

It can be concluded that the spatial and temporal variability of residents' travel flows across weekdays and weekends, extracted from GPS trajectories data, assist transport mangers to achieve superior understanding for regenerative urban and transportation planning [7].

Summary

As the concluding statement for this section, taxi GPS trajectories and SCD present accurate spatial-temporal data sources for discovering urban travel behaviour. With findings focused on the spatial and temporal similarities in human movements, it is highly functional to perform transportation and urban planning processes (Figure 3.4).

Table 3.2 Big data collection tools for travel behaviour analysis

Tools	Taxi GPS trajectories	Smart Card Data
Type of data	• Spatial, temporal	• Spatial, temporal
Features extracted	• Time of pick-up and drop-off points	• Travel time (boarding time, alight time)
	• Location (latitude, longitude) of pick-up and drop-off locations	• Locations of origin and destination
	• Speed of vehicles	
Data process method	• Spatial and temporal similarities in pick-up and drop-off points	• Spatial and temporal similarities in travel time, origin and destination

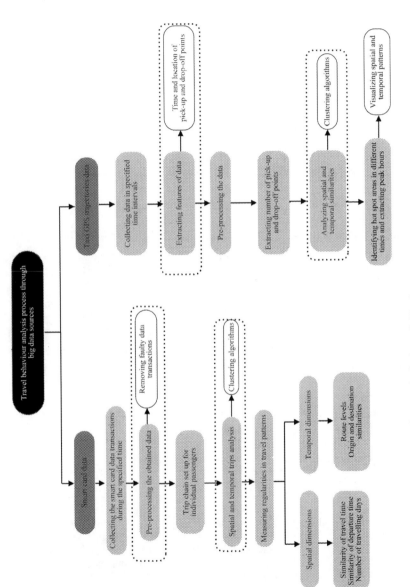

Figure 3.4 Process of travel behaviour analysis through big data sources

Data-Driven Traffic and Transportation Analysis of Beijing

Background

Beijing has a monocentric structure. The city's traffic network is a combination of several radial highways. The Beijing Urban Master Plan for 2016 to 2035 explains that the developed urban structure contains the central area, the inner suburban area and the outer suburban area. The city centre area points out to the central functional area of the capital, containing Forbidden City, the old city centre and the areas located within the 4th Ring Road. The inner suburban area covers the areas positioned between the 4th and 6th Ring Road. In these areas, six suburban new towns have been recently developed. The outer suburban area refers to the areas located outside of the 6th Ring Road [14]. Figure 3.5 indicates the spatial structure of Beijing and highlights these areas.

The public transport system of Beijing consists of buses, subways, taxis and bicycles. Although subways are Beijing's prevailing public transportation, taxis also play a vital part in ground transportation. This is because flexible routes are offered by taxis and this mode is more time-efficient and functional in intra-urban transportation than the other modes. In China, taxi trajectories provide a considerable data source for urban studies, given their capacity to capture a large proportion of urban passenger flows [41]. Therefore, taxi trajectories data as the spatial-temporal big data source were used for travel behaviour and traffic pattern analysis in this section.

Big Data Sources

Taxi GPS Trajectories

The utilized dataset[2] consist of the GPS trajectories of 10,357 taxis from the 2nd to 8th of February 2008 (Saturday to Friday) within Beijing. Each point contains features such as taxi id, date, time, longitude and latitude [55, 56].

Methodology and Process of Data Analysis

The procedure of traffic and transportation regeneration through big data sources include taxi GPS trajectories that were implemented based on the following steps for Beijing. Firstly, GPS trajectories of 10,357 taxis in text format (a CSV file) were integrated together as a primary input. The total number of points in this dataset was originally about 18 million points but after pre-processing, around 16 million points were fixed for analysis. The

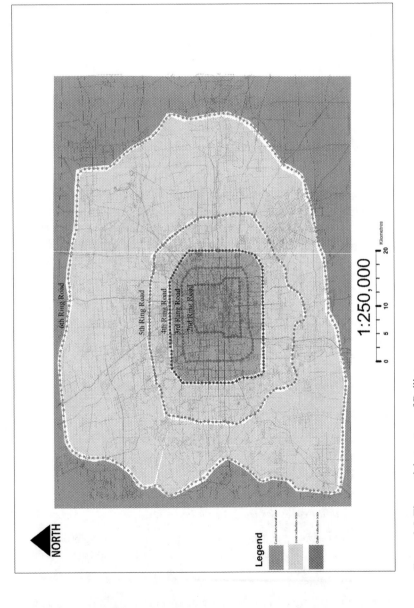

Figure 3.5 The spatial structure of Beijing

trajectory of each taxi was extracted in one-hour intervals and in a 1x1 kilometre grid. Two types of holistic and spatial-temporal analysis were done for finding the patterns of taxi movements. In the holistic analysis, the general trend of movement was determined based on the number of GPS data counts for one week. In the spatial analysis, pre-processed points were imported into the time-space cube for further investigation in ArcGIS software (Figure 3.6).

The space-time cube is a data visualization method that demonstrates spatiotemporal data inside a cube (sometimes called an 'aquarium'). This concept was originally proposed by Hägerstrand in the early 1970s in his seminal paper on time geography and has since been primarily applied to show geospatial data. The space-time cube representation has been then proposed as a tool in spatiotemporal visualization. The recent applications of this representation include geospatial visualization purposes [57] where it assigns to a three-dimensional (3D) Euclidean space. This includes a 2D geographical space as the base and the time as the height. Through this technique, residents' behaviour and interaction trajectories can be visualized across space and time [58].

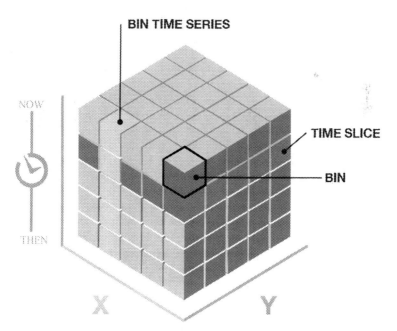

Figure 3.6 Space-time cube sample[3]

A generalized space-time cube is a conceptual representation that aids temporal data visualization techniques in general [59] and is effectively used to indicate data about spatial movements and interactions, that is, changes of spatial properties of persistent separate objects [60]. An alternative visual representation is the Space-Time-Cube (STC), which is the most distinguished element in Hägerstrand's space-time model. The STC combines time and space where time can be represented as continuous or discrete. The X- and Y-axes show the 2D space, while the time units along the Z-axis can be years, days, hours, etc. [61].

Progressively, hotspot and cold spot patterns and the holistic trend of taxi trips were extracted in the spatial scale and from the space-time cube for one week. Based on the obtained patterns and hotspot region, design solutions were proposed for developing a balance in the distribution of traffic patterns and controlling traffic congestion (Figure 3.7).

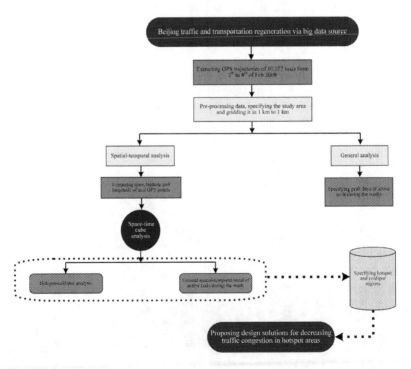

Figure 3.7 Beijing traffic and transportation regeneration process via big data source

Data Analysis and Results

Holistic Analysis

The holistic analysis made from the number of active taxis discovered the patterns of taxi travels in Beijing during the study period. It shows that although Saturday and Sunday are weekends in Beijing, the number of active taxis in these days is significant. Monday (the first weekday) constitutes the maximum number of taxi trips. This has, then, a decreasing trend and reaches to its minimum on Friday (Figure 3.8).

Space-Time Cube Analysis

• Spatial general trend.

The spatial pattern indicates that taxi movements in the central urban area of Beijing (the area located in the 5th Ring Road) drops from the first day of the week until its end. On the contrary, taxi movements in urban areas which are located outside of the 5th Ring Road increases towards the end of the week. This fact reveals that the central area of Beijing is mainly

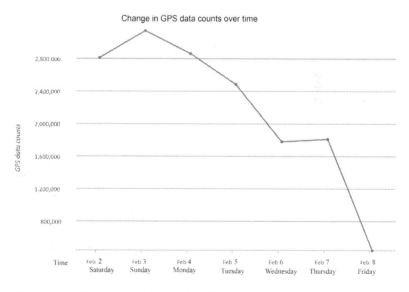

Figure 3.8 Holistic trend of changes in GPS data during the study period (2 Feb–8 Feb, 2008)

dedicated to business activities and zones in light of the number of taxi travels during the weekdays. Furthermore, the areas out of the 6th Ring Road are mostly allocated to the residential and leisure zones in view of taxi travels increasing towards the weekend (Figure 3.9).

Hotspot and Cold Spot Analysis

Figure 3.10 indicates the map of emerging hotspot analysis, integrated with time using spatial panel data. The new tool 'Emerging Hot Spot Analysis' in ArcGIS helps recognize trends in clustering point densities or summary fields in a space-time cube and in the grid of 1x1 km. The term hotspot explains a high value region in comparison with its surrounding [62]. We describe the hotspot, here, as an area that exhibits statistically significant clustering in the spatial pattern of GPS taxi points.

The analysis shows that the centre of Beijing is generally considered as the hotspot area whereas a large proportion is a diminishing hotspot (the area within the 4th Ring Road). It means that this location is a statistically significant hotspot for more than five days in a week (>90%). In addition, the intensity of clustering of high counts in each time step is decreasing. It can be inferred that this region is allocated to business, urban services and commercial areas and is a travel attraction centre during the week.

Some regions between the 4th and 5th Ring Roads were found as the oscillating hotspots. It means that there are some areas which are cold spots during weekdays but are hotspots towards weekends. It can be inferred that these regions are more cultural and recreational centres which attract more trips towards weekends. Some areas between the 4th and 5th Ring Roads were allocated as sporadic hotspots. It shows the locations that are on-again then off-again hotspots. These areas are hotspots less than five days of a week. Overall, it can be concluded that the regions allocated to hotspot areas are concentrated in the city centre and focal points of urban commutes for more than five days in a week.

On the other hand, the urban areas, located between the 5th and 6th Ring Roads, are cold spot regions. A remarkable area of this region is a diminishing cold spot. These are the locations which are cold spots five days in a week, including the last days of the week. In addition, the intensity of clustering of low counts in each time step decreases and this decrease is statistically significant. A small area of these cold spot regions was found as the persistent cold spot. This region is a cold spot five days in a week with no discernible trend, indicating an increase or decrease in the intensity of clustering of counts over time. Furthermore, some regions north and south of the cold spot region are allocated to a sporadic cold spot, a location that is an on-again then off-again cold spot. Less than five days in a week are statistically significant cold spots and there is no hotspot.

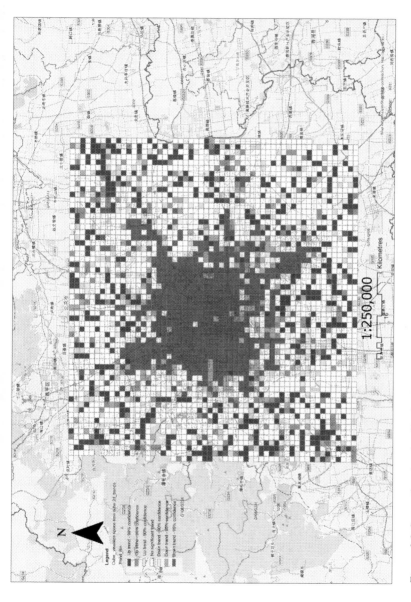

Figure 3.9 Space-time trends of taxi patterns

A small part of the cold spot region was identified as an oscillating cold spot, which means a statistically significant cold spot for the final time-step interval that has a history of also being a statistically significant hotspot during a prior time step. It can be concluded that the identified cold spot areas are not the land uses which attract people during the week. Therefore, the demand for travel is less than other areas of this region.

Design Solutions

Based on the hotspot and cold spot analyses and the holistic trend of taxi pattern movements in Beijing, the distribution of most of the trips are concentrated in the centre of Beijing. This finding is due to the unbalanced distribution of land uses and urban services which are centralized in this part of the city. Consequently, this issue leads to the concentration of traffic and congestion in this area. Some design solutions are, hence, proposed for alleviating the traffic congestion problem in the areas recognized as hotspot areas (Figure 3.11).

• Expanding metro networks.

Since metro transit prevails Beijing's public transportation, the expansion of metro networks can be effective for convincing people to use this type of public transportation compared to taxis. Based on the holistic spatial trend of taxi movements (Figure 3.9), hotspot and cold spot analysis (Figure 3.10) and the existing situation of metro networks in Beijing (Figure 3.12), 400 km of new metro paths are proposed in the hotspot regions and in the regions towards the 6th Ring Road, in which the number of travels are significantly increased toward the end of the week. The proposed new metro paths are not only effective for the continuity and connectivity of metro networks, but they can also provide access to all suburbs around (Figure 3.13).

• Shifting the monocentric spatial structure to the polycentric.

Based on the hotspot and cold spot analysis, it was identified that the congested regions are in the centre of city and the most hotspot areas are concentrated within the 1st to the 5th Ring Roads (Figure 3.11). Therefore, Beijing is obviously a monocentric city in terms of its spatial structure where approximately most of the services and business areas are centralized in one region (Figure 3.14). This issue, as previously mentioned, leads to creating a high-level traffic jam. Alternatively, it is proposed to shift the existing monocentric structure to the polycentric plan and expand the urban services and business and commercial areas. Multiple urban centres can

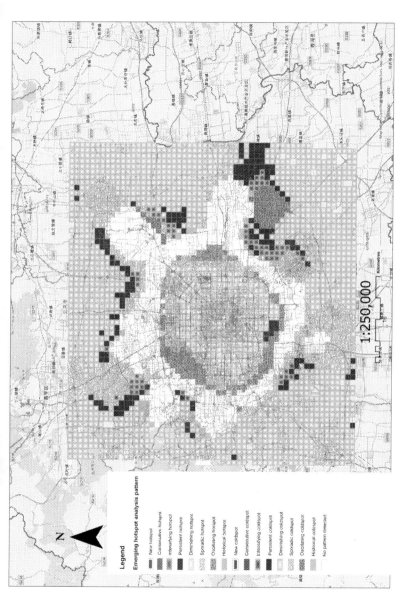

Figure 3.10 Space-time hotspot and cold spot analysis

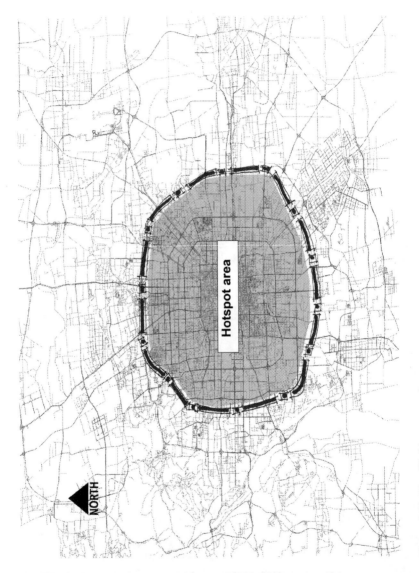

Figure 3.11 Identified hotspot regions

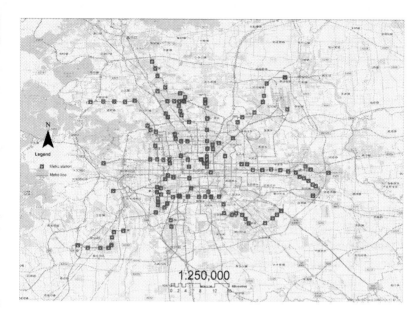

Figure 3.12 Existing metro networks

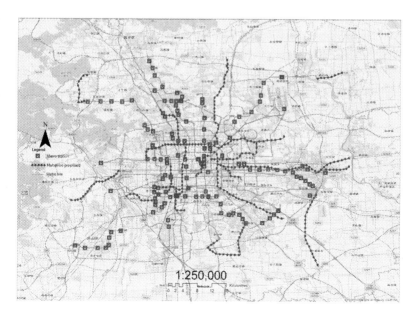

Figure 3.13 Proposed metro networks

be established for creating a balance in the level of urban services and disperse the traffic congestion. The polycentric spatial configuration is generally defined as more than an activity centre cluster in an urban area and it is commonly accepted as an opposite spatial form of the monocentricity [63]. Furthermore, developing multiple independent centres provides more equal opportunities for citizens' business and economic activities [64] (Figure 3.15).

• Restriction on private car commutes to hotspot regions.

According to the hotspot and cold spot map, the regions up to the 5th Ring Road are the main business areas and the concentrated points of most intra-city trips. Hence, it is recommended to restrict the commutes of private cars to these regions during weekdays and decrease the traffic congestion (Figure 3.16). Moreover, some public parking spots should be provided adjacent to the restricted areas.

• Development of the green transportation (walking area and bicycle lines).

Another solution for controlling the traffic in the hotspot regions is providing green transportation infrastructures. Developing interconnected pedestrian networks (Figure 3.17) integrated with interconnected cycling networks (Figure 3.18) can be effective strategies to lift the traffic pressures from the city centre and its main roads.

Conclusion

Understanding the traffic patterns through spatial and temporal analysis can be crucial for regenerative urban planning and transportation solutions for overcrowded cities like Beijing. Therefore, this chapter presented the applications, advantages and disadvantages of the wide range of big data technologies including GPS trajectories, SCD and social media in urban traffic and transportation analysis and tested the application of taxi GPS trajectories for identifying the traffic behaviour and patterns of Beijing. It was identified that taxi GPS trajectories and movements as one of the important types of public transportation in Beijing can present the traffic patterns in this city. Furthermore, space-time analysis of these movements through big data sources can reflect the hotspot and cold spot regions, and origins and destinations of travels. As a result, it was found out that these types of big data technologies and analyses enable urban planners and designers to

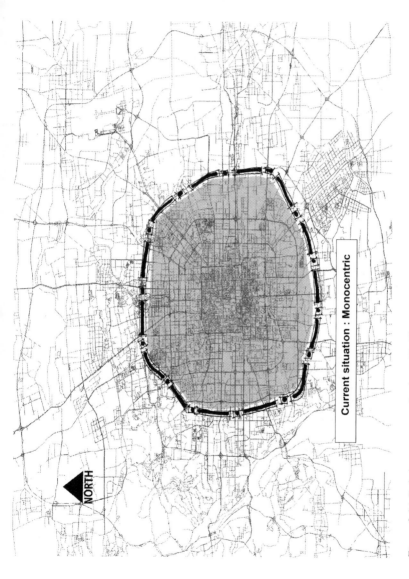

Current situation : Monocentric

NORTH

Figure 3.14 Existing monocentric plan of Beijing

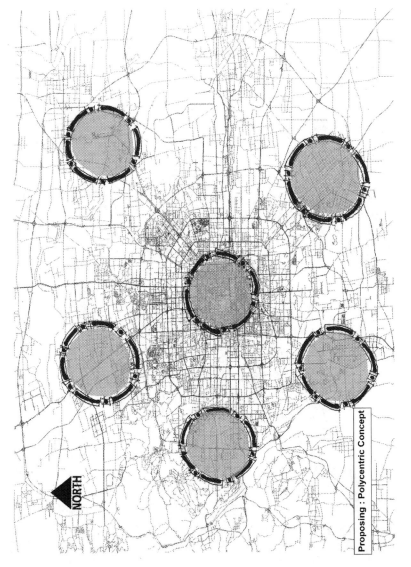

Figure 3.15 Proposed polycentric plan for Beijing

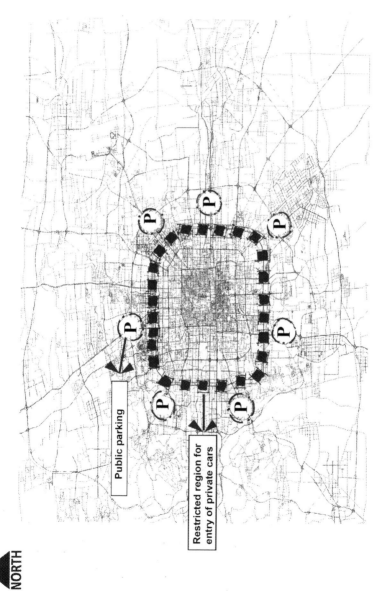

NORTH

Public parking

Restricted region for entry of private cars

Figure 3.16 Restricted areas for private car commutes

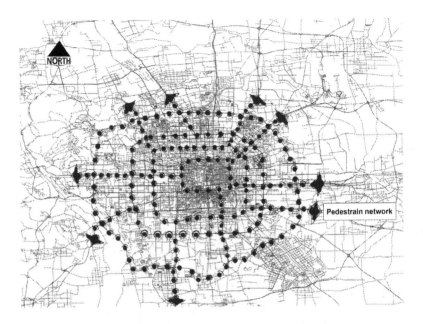

Figure 3.17 Proposed pedestrian networks in the hotspot regions

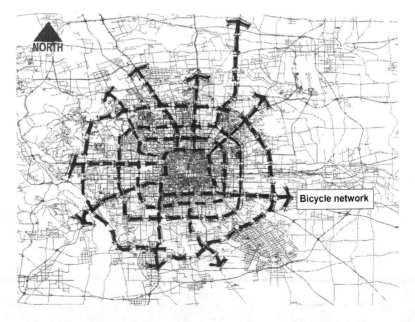

Figure 3.18 Proposed cycling networks in the hotspot regions

achieve insight regarding the traffic patterns and focal points of the city and plan for bespoke design solutions and traffic control strategies.

Notes

1 https://uym.ibb.gov.tr/
2 Beijing City Lab, 2013, Data 4, 1 T-Drive Taxi Trajectories. www.beijingcitylab. com
3 https://desktop.arcgis.com/en/arcmap/latest/tools/space-time-pattern-mining-toolbox/create-space-time-cube.htm

References

1 Liu, L., et al. Understanding individual and collective mobility patterns from smart card records: A case study in Shenzhen. In *2009 12th International IEEE Conference on Intelligent Transportation Systems*. 2009. IEEE.
2 Farahani, R.Z., et al., A review of urban transportation network design problems. *European Journal of Operational Research*, 2013. **229**(2): p. 281–302.
3 Chen, B.Y. and W.H. Lam, Smart transportation: Theory and practice. *Journal of Advanced Transportation*, 2016. **50**(2): p. 141–144.
4 Guerrero-Ibáñez, J., S. Zeadally, and J. Contreras-Castillo, Sensor technologies for intelligent transportation systems. *Sensors*, 2018. **18**(4): p. 1212.
5 Yang, J. and J. Ma. A big-data processing framework for uncertainties in transportation data. In *2015 IEEE International Conference on Fuzzy Systems (FUZZ-IEEE)*. 2015. IEEE.
6 Ram, S., et al. SMARTBUS: A web application for smart urban mobility and transportation. In *Proceedings of the 25th International Conference Companion on World Wide Web*. 2016. International World Wide Web Conferences Steering Committee.
7 Tang, J., et al., Uncovering urban human mobility from large scale taxi GPS data. *Physica A: Statistical Mechanics and Its Applications*, 2015. **438**: p. 140–153.
8 Farooq, A., et al., Transportation planning through GIS and multicriteria analysis: Case study of Beijing and Xiong'an. *Journal of Advanced Transportation*, 2018. **2018**.
9 Chatterjee, A. and M.M. Venigalla, Travel demand forecasting for urban transportation planning. *Handbook of Transportation Engineering*, 2004. **1**.
10 Meyer, M.D., Transport planning for urban areas: A retrospective look and future prospects. *Journal of Advanced Transportation*, 2000. **34**(1): p. 143–171.
11 *International Conference on Contemporary Affairs in Architecture and Urbanism* (ICCAUA-2019) 9–10 May 2019, ICCAUA 2019 Conference Proceedings, AHEP University, Alanya, Turkey.
12 Hao, J., J. Zhu, and R. Zhong, The rise of big data on urban studies and planning practices in China: Review and open research issues. *Journal of Urban Management*, 2015. **4**(2): p. 92–124.
13 Graells-Garrido, E., D. Caro, and D. Parra, Inferring modes of transportation using mobile phone data. *EPJ Data Science*, 2018. **7**(1): p. 49.

14 Zhao, P. and H. Hu, Geographical patterns of traffic congestion in growing megacities: Big data analytics from Beijing. *Cities*, 2019. **92**: p. 164–174.

15 Zhang, K., et al., Analyzing spatiotemporal congestion pattern on urban roads based on taxi GPS data. *Journal of Transport and Land Use*, 2017. **10**(1): p. 675–694.

16 Segura-Garcia, J., et al., Low-cost alternatives for urban noise nuisance monitoring using wireless sensor networks. *IEEE Sensors Journal*, 2014. **15**(2): p. 836–844.

17 Liu, Y., et al., Grid mapping for spatial pattern analyses of recurrent urban traffic congestion based on taxi GPS sensing data. *Sustainability*, 2017. **9**(4): p. 533.

18 Xu, S., S. Li, and R. Wen, Sensing and detecting traffic events using geosocial media data: A review. *Computers, Environment and Urban Systems*, 2018. **72**: p. 146–160.

19. Ma, Q. and K. Kockelman, A low-cost GPS-data-enhanced approach for traffic network evaluations. *International Journal of Intelligent Transportation Systems Research*, 2019. **17**(1): p. 9–17.

20 D'Andrea, E. and F. Marcelloni, Detection of traffic congestion and incidents from GPS trace analysis. *Expert Systems with Applications*, 2017. **73**: p. 43–56.

21. Liu, Y., et al., Grid mapping for spatial pattern analyses of recurrent urban traffic congestion based on taxi GPS sensing data. *Sustainability*, 2017. **9**(4): p. 533.

22 Soe, N.C., T.L.L. Thein, and T. Aung. GPS tracking and traffic monitoring system in urban transportation. In *2018 IEEE 7th Global Conference on Consumer Electronics (GCCE)*. 2018. IEEE.

23 Rahman, M.M., et al. Traffic pattern analysis from GPS data: A case study of Dhaka City. In *2018 IEEE International Conference on Electronics, Computing and Communication Technologies (CONECCT)*. 2018. IEEE.

24. Stipancic, J., et al., Measuring and visualizing space – time congestion patterns in an urban road network using large-scale smartphone-collected GPS data. *Transportation Letters*, 2019. **11**(7): p. 391–401.

25 Wang, Y., et al. Mining traffic congestion correlation between road segments on GPS trajectories. In *2016 IEEE International Conference on Smart Computing (SMARTCOMP)*. 2016. IEEE.

26. Zhang, K., et al., Analyzing spatiotemporal congestion pattern on urban roads based on taxi GPS data. *Journal of Transport and Land Use*, 2017. **10**(1): p. 675–694.

27 Ma, Q. and K.J.I.J.o.I.T.S.R. Kockelman, A low-cost GPS-data-enhanced approach for traffic network evaluations. *International Journal of Intelligent Transportation Systems Research*, 2019. **17**(1): p. 9–17.

28 Stipancic, J., et al., Measuring and visualizing space – time congestion patterns in an urban road network using large-scale smartphone-collected GPS data. *Transportation Letters*, 2019. **11**(7): p. 391–401.

29 Lian, J. and L. Zhang. One-month Beijing taxi GPS trajectory dataset with taxi IDs and vehicle status. In *Proceedings of the First Workshop on Data Acquisition to Analysis*. 2018.

30 Al-qaness, M.A., et al. Real-time traffic congestion analysis based on collected Tweets. In *2019 IEEE International Conferences on Ubiquitous Computing &*

Communications (IUCC) and Data Science and Computational Intelligence (DSCI) and Smart Computing, Networking and Services (SmartCNS). 2019. IEEE.

31 Kumari, S., et al., Real-time detection of traffic from Twitter stream analysis. *International Research Journal of Engineering and Technology,* 2016. **3**(4): p. 2350–2354.

32 D'Andrea, E., et al., Real-time detection of traffic from Twitter stream analysis. *IEEE Transactions on Intelligent Transportation Systems,* 2015. **16**(4): p. 2269–2283.

33 Zulfikar, M.T., Detection traffic congestion based on Twitter data using machine learning. *Procedia Computer Science,* 2019. **157**: p. 118–124.

34 Dabiri, S. and K. Heaslip, Developing a Twitter-based traffic event detection model using deep learning architectures. *Expert Systems with Applications,* 2019. **118**: p. 425–439.

35 Gu, Y., Z.S. Qian, and F. Chen, From Twitter to detector: Real-time traffic incident detection using social media data. *Transportation Research Part C: Emerging Technologies,* 2016. **67**: p. 321–342.

36 Zhang, Z., et al. Extraction of traffic information from social media interactions: Methods and experiments. In *17th International IEEE Conference on Intelligent Transportation Systems (ITSC14) Institute of Electrical and Electronics Engineers (IEEE) China Association of Automation Qingdao Academy of Intelligent Industries State Key Laboratory of Management and Control for Complex Systems Xi'an Jiaotong University, China Institute of Automation, Chinese Academy of Sciences.* 2014.

37 Alomari, E. and R. Mehmood. Analysis of Tweets in Arabic language for detection of road traffic conditions. In *International Conference on Smart Cities, Infrastructure, Technologies and Applications.* 2017. Springer.

38 Toole, J.L., et al., The path most traveled: Travel demand estimation using big data resources. *Transportation Research Part C: Emerging Technologies,* 2015. **58**: p. 162–177.

39 Calabrese, F., et al., Understanding individual mobility patterns from urban sensing data: A mobile phone trace example. *Transportation Research Part C: Emerging Technologies,* 2013. **26**: p. 301–313.

40 Wang, Z., S.Y. He, and Y. Leung, Applying mobile phone data to travel behaviour research: A literature review. *Travel Behaviour and Society,* 2018. **11**: p. 141–155.

41 Wang, H., et al., Revealing spatial-temporal characteristics and patterns of urban travel: A large-scale analysis and visualization study with taxi GPS data. *ISPRS International Journal of Geo-Information,* 2019. **8**(6): p. 257.

42 Medina, S.A.O., Inferring weekly primary activity patterns using public transport smart card data and a household travel survey. *Travel Behaviour and Society,* 2018. **12**: p. 93–101.

43 Chakirov, A. and A. Erath, Use of public transport smart card fare payment data for travel behaviour analysis in Singapore. *Arbeitsberichte/IVT,* 2011. **729**.

44 Zhao, J., et al., Spatio-temporal analysis of passenger travel patterns in massive smart card data. *IEEE Transactions on Intelligent Transportation Systems,* 2017. **18**(11): p. 3135–3146.

45 Ma, X., et al., Mining smart card data for transit riders' travel patterns. *Transportation Research Part C: Emerging Technologies*, 2013. **36**: p. 1–12.

46 Ali, A., J. Kim, and S. Lee, Travel behavior analysis using smart card data. *KSCE Journal of Civil Engineering*, 2016. **20**(4): p. 1532–1539.

47 Ouyang, Q., et al., Passenger travel regularity analysis based on a large scale smart card data. *Journal of Advanced Transportation*, 2018. **2018**.

48. Ma, X., et al., Understanding commuting patterns using transit smart card data. *Journal of Transport Geography*, 2017. **58**: p. 135–145.

49 Liu, X., et al., Spatial variation of taxi demand using GPS trajectories and POI data. *Journal of Advanced Transportation*, 2020. **2020**.

50 Zhang, H., et al., Detecting taxi travel patterns using GPS trajectory data: A case study of Beijing. *KSCE Journal of Civil Engineering*, 2019. **23**(4): p. 1797–1805.

51 Zheng, L., et al., Spatial – temporal travel pattern mining using massive taxi trajectory data. *Physica A: Statistical Mechanics and its Applications*, 2018. **501**: p. 24–41.

52 Jiang, W., et al. A multi-period analysis of taxi drivers' behaviors based on GPS trajectories. In *2017 IEEE 20th International Conference on Intelligent Transportation Systems (ITSC)*. 2017. IEEE.

53 Wei, M., Y. Liu, and T.J. Sigler. An exploratory analysis of Brisbane's commuter travel patterns using smart card data. In *Proceedings of the State of Australian Cities Research Network; State of Australian Cities National Conference, Gold Coast, Australia*. 2015.

54 Hu, X., S. An, and J. Wang, Taxi driver's operation behavior and passengers' demand analysis based on GPS data. *Journal of Advanced Transportation*, 2018. **2018**.

55 Yuan, J., et al. Driving with knowledge from the physical world. In *Proceedings of the 17th ACM SIGKDD International Conference on Knowledge discovery and Data Mining*. 2011.

56 Yuan, J., et al. T-drive: Driving directions based on taxi trajectories. In *Proceedings of the 18th SIGSPATIAL International Conference on Advances in Geographic Information Systems*. 2010.

57 Kristensson, P.O., et al., An evaluation of space time cube representation of spatiotemporal patterns. *Ieee Transactions on Visualization and Computer Graphics*, 2008. **15**(4): p. 696–702.

58 Fang, T.B. and Y. Lu, Constructing a near real-time space-time cube to depict urban ambient air pollution scenario. *Transactions in GIS*, 2011. **15**(5): p. 635–649.

59 Bach, B., et al. A descriptive framework for temporal data visualizations based on generalized space-time cubes. In *Computer Graphics Forum*. 2017. Wiley Online Library.

60 Gatalsky, P., N. Andrienko, and G. Andrienko. Interactive analysis of event data using space-time cube. In *Proceedings Eighth International Conference on Information Visualisation, 2004. IV 2004*. 2004. IEEE.

61 Li, X., A. Çöltekin, and M.-J. Kraak. Visual exploration of eye movement data using the space-time-cube. In *International Conference on Geographic Information Science*. 2010. Springer.

62 Isobe, A., et al., East Asian seas: A hot spot of pelagic microplastics. *Marine Pollution Bulletin*, 2015. **101**(2): p. 618–623.

63 Sat, N.A., Monocentric or polycentric? Defining morphological structure of NUTS-2 regions of Turkey from 2000 to 2016. *Geographica Pannonica*, 2018. **22**(1).

64 Wang, M., Polycentric urban development and urban amenities: Evidence from Chinese cities. *Environment and Planning B: Urban Analytics and City Science*, 2021. **48**(3): p. 400–416.

4 Big Data and Urban Environmental Sustainability

Urban Environmental Issues and Impacts on Planning Approach

The pollution level of the environment is aggravated as cities become industrialized [1]. Air pollution and noise pollution are the most detrimental pollution types which impact the quality of life in urban areas and increase with the fast urbanization development. Air pollution imposes drastic physical (heart disease, lung cancer, chronic respiratory diseases) and psychological health effects (depression and risk of suicide) on citizens [2]. Likewise, noise pollution leads to sleep disturbance, cardiovascular diseases and hearing loss [3] and influences on human behaviour and their performance [4].

Thus, effective environmental planning practices are required for controlling these pollutions. Environmental planning is defined as the process of making proper time and spatial arrangements relating to people's activities and environments according to social, economic and ecological principles in order to obtain a more sustainable built environment [5].

Urban environmental planning is, generally, a substantial dynamic procedure for urban sustainability [6] in which monitoring the pollution is its first main step. Actually, in the large scale, environmental monitoring is a vital project to control climate change and global warming [4] while in the small scale, the surveillance and management of environmental pollution is fundamental to the development of modern metropolitan urban areas [5].

Urban environmental planning should actively engage citizens during all steps of the planning and implementation processes [6]. Big data technology can significantly improve the participation of residents in environmental monitoring and developing effective measures for decreasing pollutants in urban areas. Next to the monitoring task, it is necessary to create a change in urban structure for reducing the pollutants. It is generally argued that spatial factors such as urban spatial structures, land uses, spatial forms,

DOI: 10.4324/9781003139942-4

transportation, and green spaces in urban planning can effect on the concentration level of air and noise pollutants in urban precincts [7]. As a result, the correlation of these factors with the amount of pollutants in these areas can be analyzed in order to control the level of pollution and regenerate the urban structure.

Big Data for Air Pollution Control

Background

Air pollution is one of the serious issues which irritate and impact urban residents' health, particularly in developing countries with their unprecedented population growth [8, 9]. As a consequence, it is necessary to avoid aggravation of the air pollution and control it via proper monitoring regimes [10]. Air Quality Index (AQI) is one of the effective monitors of the level of air pollution [10] and its ambient pollutants. This index encompasses various pollutants such as So2, No2, Co, PM 2.5,[1] Airborne Particulate Matter (APM) [11] and Suspended Particulate Matter (SPM). In this section, big data technology application is explained for monitoring air pollution through the fixed stations, WSNs and social media data.

Fixed Stations

Fixed stations for monitoring air pollution are the first generation of applying big data technology for monitoring the air quality and the continuous measurement of the most important pollutants. Due to the fact that installation costs are high and these stations generally require a large space for construction, the number of fixed stations are limited in urban precincts and the deployment density is relatively low [12, 13]. Moreover, these sites are regularly managed by government agencies and/or independent authorities [14]. The obtained data from fixed stations are accurate, precise and highly reliable [15]. However, these stations are bulky, costly and inflexible [15, 16], need land and skilled technicians to maintain [8] and human resources and money to manage [10].

Through the fixed stations application, various ambient pollutants and AQI are monitored in each second or minute interval and updated on an hourly or daily basis [14]. The obtained data are reported and visualized online through the website, smartphones and/or large LCDs which are set up in cities. Fixed monitoring stations are only able to measure the air pollution within a specific region, and raw data, aggregated from these stations, are used to extrapolate the density of pollutants throughout the whole region using dispersion models [2] (Figure 4.1).

Figure 4.1 Fixed station for monitoring air pollution and a large LCD for its reporting

Wireless Sensor Network (WSN)

The application of WSNs for air pollution monitoring can be categorized in three types: static sensor networks (the sensor nodes regularly installed on streetlights, traffic light poles and walls), community sensor networks (carried by users) and vehicle sensor networks (carried by public transportation like buses or taxis) [15]. Features which are extracted for monitoring are the amount of pollutants including Co, Co2, No2 and PM and the information regarding the location, time and date [9, 17].

Measuring air pollution through WSNs has the following process. The air pollution information is, first, sensed through sensors. In some situations, a data algorithm is used to unify the data, omit the repetitive data and filter the invalid ones to save energy [18]. Data are then sent to servers through the sync nodes collecting time and location information, compiling the database and getting the data processed via the control centre [14, 17, 19, 20]. In the next step, signals are continuously transformed to digital numbers by digital convertors [21–24]. The obtained pollution level is, hence, compared with the standard level and transformed to the pollution status as AQI [13]. Finally, people and residents are informed regarding the identified pollution level through GPRS system, SMS, email, large displays all over a city [19, 22, 23], mobile or web-based visualizations [14, 22, 25] and/or by statistical techniques such as tables and line graphs [13, 18].

Using the WSNs for monitoring the air pollution has some advantages:

- This system is inexpensive [26] and powerful for air pollution monitoring [22],
- It is a simple tool [23, 27] and facilitates immediate monitoring [18],
- It can be conveniently developed and controlled from long distances [19],
- The air quality prediction is possible as to constructing the predictive models based on historical data [19],
- This technology benefits from the short monitoring time intervals [18].

On the other hand, there are some challenges in applying WSNs:

- The constant provision of energy sources and power is one of the main issues in continuously monitoring air pollution [9, 22, 28],
- WSN requires a wide coverage area [16, 20, 26],
- WSN collects a huge amount of data. As a consequence, managing this volume of data can be difficult [18].

In a nutshell, WSN is an effective tool for the real-time air pollution monitoring and its prediction, provided with a constant power source. It is also useful to identify various high-risk regions of the city and the regions in need of regular control [22]. Moreover, the air pollution issues can be communicated very conveniently [13] and authorities can make immediate actions based on the obtained data for minimizing the destructive impacts of air pollution on residents by evacuating or sending emergency response teams [2, 4].

Geo-Tagged Social Media

Social media data, as citizen-led, passive monitoring, present valuable and timely information about the public perception of air quality [2, 8]. In fact, there is a direct correlation between the volume of air quality messages and the level of air pollution. In other words, social media platforms can demonstrate the spectrum of the air pollution in urban precincts [10].

The data features from social media posts consist of content, time and geographical location. The posts about the air quality are generally accumulated during the specified time. Theses posts are collected based on the determined keywords such as air pollution, air quality, PM 2.5 and haze [11]. The dictionary of the terms relevant to the air pollution is constructed [29] and pre-processing is done through filtering the noise in posts such as advertisements, indoor air pollution data [8], eliminating the words emerging less than ten times [12] and deleting the duplicate words [11]. It is argued that among three types of social media posts such as original individual messages, re-mention (retweet) messages and mobile app messages, original individual messages have a strong relationship with the air pollutant measurements [8]. Therefore, this type is usually used for analyzing the level of air pollution. In the next step, the meaning of each post is surveyed through the various methods including Natural Language Processing (NLP) [2]. The obtained sentiments are categorized as negative, positive and neutral, manually [8, 30] or automatically with machine learning algorithms [31]. The cross-correlation analysis is, then, applied to analyze the dependence between the number of geo-located posts about air pollution and the actual data of pollutants or AQI (achieved through monitoring stations) via Pearson correlation coefficient [8, 30] or Spearman's rank correlation coefficient [30].

The research suggests that negative tweets have more strong correlation with the level of pollutants because these posts can usually convey the destructive impacts of the air pollution [8]. In some situations, machine learning methods such as Gradient Tree Boosting [8, 30], Markov Random Field [12] and ARIMA models (time series analysis model) [10] are used combined with the correlation methods to monitor and estimate the air pollutants or AQI applying the classified individual messages. Finally, the results and predicted air pollution data are verified through the actual air monitoring data, fixed stations located in proximity of the region [2, 12] or pictures attached to the posts [29].

Some advantages can be enumerated from using social media data for monitoring air pollution:

- This technology is considered as a complementary source for traditional monitoring stations to dynamically discover and identify the air pollution in high population density regions [2, 12, 29],
- Social media data are cost-effective and scalable in a real-time approach [2, 10, 12], and it does not impose the cost for maintenance, installation and deployment [29],
- It enables citizens to participate in monitoring and management of air pollution [10, 11],
- It is functional for cities which do not have air monitoring stations [30].

The social media technique has some shortcomings:

- Residents of some regions may be too digitally illiterate to share their thoughts and opinions about the air pollution in social media networks [2],
- Some poor urban and rural areas are deprived from access to the internet and therefore have limited access to the social media application [2, 11, 12],
- In some cases, the precise geographical locations derived from social media are not accurate and have errors for extracting the air pollution data [8],
- Using the social media data of some users may not be legal because they may not be aware that their messages are public and searchable [8],
- Social-cultural differences and diversity should be considered for monitoring the air pollution from these datasets since people from different countries have various expressions and slang to express their emotions about air pollution. As a result, it is laborious work to recognize those subtle differences from a huge amount of data [29],
- People have a various tolerance threshold to air pollution, so the social media posts can be unreal or biased in some situations [29],
- Some people may generate fake air pollution posts for some regions because of malicious intentions [29] or exaggerating the air pollution intensity [10].

All in all, in spite of the disadvantages for social media data, this method, as a social sensor, can be effectively used as a complementary source for discovering air pollution and reducing its subsequent impacts [2].

Summary

It can be concluded that the identified approaches for monitoring air pollution can collect the real-time patterns of the air pollution in cities. These technologies can be applied integratively to collect the amount of pollutants and AQI and provide data for scientists, policy makers and planners to make effective measures for managing and enhancing the environment [25]. Figure 4.2 and Table 4.1 present the key processes and attributes of air pollution monitoring through big data technologies.

Data-Driven Noise Management Principles

Background

Noise pollution is a growing challenge for sustainable development of urban regions in line with the growth and development of cities [32]. The European Noise Directive (END) defines the environmental noise as 'unwanted or harmful outdoor sound created by human activities, such as noise emanated through transport, road traffic, rail traffic, air traffic, and from sites of

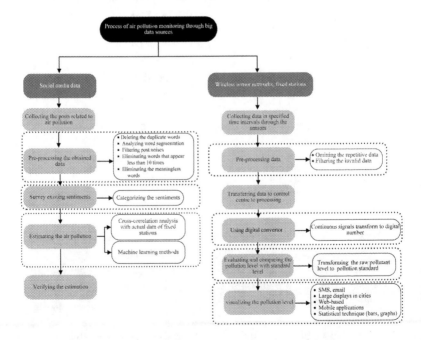

Figure 4.2 Process of air pollution monitoring through big data sources

Table 4.1 Big data tools for air pollution monitoring

Tools	Fixed stations	Wireless Sensor Networks (WSNs)	Geo-tagged social media data
Types of data	Spatial, temporal	Spatial, temporal	Spatial, temporal, descriptive
Features extracted	Location, time and the amount of pollutants	Location, time and the amount of pollutants	Location, time and content of posts
The analysis process	Process and visualization in tables, graphs and maps, public awareness with mobile phone applications, web pages and large LCD displays		Analysis of posts and finding coefficient among the reported and actual air pollution data

industrial activity' [4]. The noise level is estimated as the equivalent continuous sound level or Leq, calculated in decibels (dB) over a time interval [33]. Monitoring noise pollution has evolved with the development of technology and emerging smart methods. In this section, the technique of big data technology is explained for noise pollution monitoring through mobile phone applications and WSNs.

Mobile Phone Application for Noise Monitoring

The increasing popularity of smart mobile phones has led to making smart applications ubiquitous everywhere. Hence, various means of environmental monitoring in sound measurement applications [3], including Ear Phone, Noise Tube [34] and NoiseSPY [35], have provided a great platform for noise monitoring data collection [36] and for reinforcing the spatial and temporal coverages of space sensing [37]. Some powerful sensors are embedded in smartphones such as microphones, cameras and GPS receivers and are used for noise monitoring [36] and discovering the sound power of the surrounding environment [32, 37, 38]. Mobile phones can be, therefore, considered as active noise sensors [39] in urban analysis.

With this respect, ambient noises can be measured in a second through mobile phones. It needs to involve volunteers to follow pre-defined routes or regions in a specified time. The accuracy of a noise map has a straight link with the number of volunteers and location of sampled data [3]. Participants should hold the mobile phones in a proper position for obtaining the precise sound samples [38]. Firstly, data are pre-processed in mobile phones and transferred to a centralized place and cloud server for extra processing, data geo-referencing and visualization via web portals [3, 6, 33, 37]. As a result of this method, a collective noise map is created [33]. During this process, the voltages which are sensed by the microphones are turned to a noise level through a weighting filter equivalent to noise level per second [33–35, 37] or signal processing algorithms. Thus, this process leads to a group of measurements which are presented on the screen as numerical factors and on histograms [39]. The mobile application changes the recorded sound pressures and displays the equivalent Sound Pressure Level (SPL) (Leq) in dB secondly [3]. However, it should be considered that microphones of smartphones should be calibrated before any measurement [36] to achieve precise noise data [37]. The calibration in this case is a comparative process by which the measurement readings are compared with those of reliable, reference devices (compared with values obtained by a professional sound level meter) and enhances the device precision and the degree of proximity to the correct values [34, 40].

The geographical coordinates of noise levels are tagged through GPS receivers and the map matching algorithms are applied for GPS positioning. Accordingly, the sources of noises and sounds (e.g., cars, airplanes, construction), intensity and subjective evaluation of sounds (loud, annoying) are identified through social tagging [39]. Overall, four types of features including time, location (GPS coordinates), loudness level and the sound feature can be extracted for further analysis [33, 38]. Finally, the obtained measurements are classified as:

1) Less than 60 dB: green/no risk,
2) From 60 dB to 70 dB: yellow/annoying,
3) From 70 dB to 80 dB: orange/alarm,
4) More than 80 dB: red/risky,

[41] and visualized through colour maps [34]. Due to the fact that covering the entire parts of a region is a very difficult task, it is necessary to apply a spatial interpolation approach such as Kriging, linear regression and nearest neighbour methods [32] to obtain the full coverage of the area and make an accurate noise map [3]. This can be generated through ArcGIS software [32, 42].

The obtained map can be validated through various methods such as descriptive statistics techniques, making comparisons with real sound level measurements at distinct points [34] and by the manual review and interview with participants [35]. In some applications in smartphones, digital questionnaires can be surveyed from users to collect perceptual data on the noise level [6].

The main benefits of this method are:

- It is an inexpensive [4, 35], convenient and quick solution for noise monitoring [6, 32] and provides an easy platform for citizens' participation [39],
- This is useful for small cities which do not have monitoring systems [39],
- A mobile phone is a small and economical sensor for noise monitoring [35],
- Since smartphones are ubiquitous everywhere, it facilitates the mass cooperation of residents in noise monitoring [6].

Some challenges can be mentioned for using mobile phone applications in noise monitoring:

- Smartphones with Android systems are assembled by various companies. Consequently, these devices have various microphones and audio structures. In this situation, the results of noise monitoring may be different from each other [36],
- The probable breach of personal data is a challenge here [36],
- The accuracy of measurement is lower than professional sound level meters [37],
- The calibration of a phone is a time-consuming process and it causes a high amount of workload [32],
- Wind, conversation of users or occasional disruptions lead to influence and overestimation of the sound level [34],
- Having the citizens engaged to contribute for data collection over a long period of time can be challenging [6, 34],
- Setting the mobile phone in an appropriate position is difficult for long-term data collection [32],
- The location of noise pollution may not be always recorded because GPS may get turned off in some situations [35] and data deviation may arise [6],
- Due to the fact that mobile phones should run various sensors (GPS, WIFI), providing sufficient power for continuous data collection is challenging [35].

It can be concluded that although there are challenges in applying mobile phones for noise monitoring, this method enhances the awareness of citizens regarding urban environmental issues and enables them to play an active role in collecting data and contributing towards noise pollution minimization. This method can be a low-cost complementary method for traditional noise monitoring and valuable for cities which lack fundamental infrastructures for noise monitoring.

WSNs for Noise Monitoring

WSNs can be a proper tool for collecting real-time data for noise monitoring. This technique is processed through consistent steps in specified time intervals. Data are, first, pre-processed to remove irregular values, be refined and distinguish signals. The signals from WSN microphones should be amplified. An analog to digital convertor is then employed to extract the digital values and transfer the voltages to decibels [43]. AI algorithms are used for calculating the sound pressure levels and data clustering [44]. Processed data (noise level data) are transferred to centralized nodes [45–47] for storage and further processing [48, 49]. Furthermore, noise pollution values include GPS data and location information of sensors. Hence, the peak hours of noise pollution and highly impacted areas can be identified via statistical analysis [50]. Finally, the processed data is visualized applying geo-spatial maps, smartphones [43] and/or a web-based database [47].

Advantages for WSNs in noise monitoring are:

- Resulting data are consistent and have a high accuracy, great granularity and reliability for noise monitoring [49, 51],
- Long-term, continuous, independent and low-cost noise monitoring is applied via WSNs [52],
- There is no need for the physical presence of an operator for noise monitoring [43] and human intervention is only required for the installation and removal of the network [49],
- The dynamic noise map is automatically generated in urban areas and its cost is therefore reduced [47].

However, the challenges are:

- Providing unlimited electric power is one of the main challenges for applying WSNs in noise monitoring [45],
- Transmission of data from sensor nodes to central servers creates a network challenge [47].

It can be concluded that WSNs can be a substitute approach for overcoming the disadvantages of the current noise data collection process [53] with the higher level of precision, simplicity and effectiveness [46].

Summary

WSNs and mobile phone applications provide smart methods for monitoring noise pollution in real-time. Although both have some drawbacks, these technologies can be effectively applied as a complementary method for traditional noise monitoring. Furthermore, both technologies directly collect human behaviour features for noise monitoring. This is called participatory sensing which is conducted by residents who are the subject of noise pollution measurements [34]. On the other hand, people are the objects in noise pollution monitoring through WSNs. Therefore, WSNs and mobile phones, both, create the direct link between data and residents' behaviour in the urban context. The obtained pattern can be used for making effective measurements in evaluating the noise pollution and planning for its reduction (Figure 4.3).

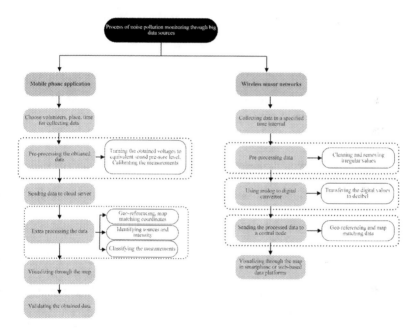

Figure 4.3 Process of noise pollution monitoring through big data sources

Table 4.2 Attributes of mobile phone applications and WSNs for noise pollution monitoring

Tools	WSNs	Mobile phone application
Type of data	Spatial, temporal	Spatial, temporal, descriptive
Extracted features	Location, time, the amount of pollution	Location, time, the amount of pollution, the sources of pollution
The process of pollution level analysis	Processing data, geo-referencing and visualization through maps and graphs	

Tehran's Urban Environmental Regeneration via Big Data Technologies

Tehran, Iran's capital city is positioned in the north with the latitude and longitude of 51°02′–51°36′ and 35°34′–35°50′, total area of 751 km, and is divided into 22 districts for urban services [54]. Tehran is the most crowded city in Iran and West Asia with 8.5 million residents [55]. Due to the fact that a large number of people commute to Tehran for work from surrounding regions, its population reaches to 12.5 million people during the days [56].

Tehran suffers from serious air pollution due to several factors. The topography and meteorological situation of this city is the issue as it is environed with mountains in the north and east which act as an obstacle for natural movement of air and trap the polluted air in the city. The second issue is the vehicles which have been manufactured with low quality and without proper environmental considerations. The third intensifying factor is the huge amount of the low quality and high polluting fuel production and consumption in transportation and manufacturing industries of the city [57]. This issue is exacerbated during the winter season as a dire consequence of atmospheric temperature inversion [56], particularly in December and January which leads to school shutdowns and a large number of hospital admissions because of cardiovascular and respiratory diseases [58].

National authorities and the Municipality of Tehran have endeavoured to reduce the air pollution in the city. For instance, laws, regulations and standards have been reconsidered and a master plan for reducing air pollution has been approved. [59]. The Air Pollution Control Department (AQCC) was founded by the Municipality of Tehran in 1933 [60] and 23 fixed stations were stablished for monitoring the concentration of air pollutants [61]. As a result of this program, the concentration of each pollutant is monitored in real time but because of a huge volume of data, the average hourly density of pollutants are calculated and reported in an Excel format [62, 63].

Among the various pollutants which are measured by the fixed stations, PM 2.5 pollutant is the most considerable pollution concern of Tehran [58]. As mentioned previously, PM 2.5 is suspended particles of less than 2.5 microns and recognized as the most hazardous air pollutant [64] because of its harmful health impacts including asthma, respiratory and cardiovascular diseases as well as destructive environmental impacts [65]. It is estimated that more than 4000 people, annually, lose their lives prematurely due to the ambient PM 2.5 air pollution [66] [58]. Figure 4.4 depicts the coverage and position of the 23 stations, of which 17 can measure the PM 2.5 concentration of the city.

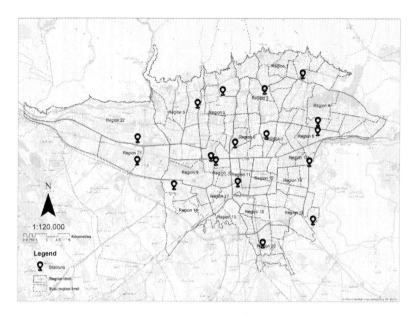

Figure 4.4 The position of stations measuring PM 2.5 pollutant in Tehran, within the 22 regions and sub-regions

Therefore, the research and development part of this chapter is focused on developing and proposing executive and regenerative urban design strategies. This analysis is to alleviate the PM 2.5 concentrations issue in Tehran's regions suffering from the high level of pollution, identified by the big data sources and obtained from the presented monitoring stations.

Methodology and Process of Data Analysis

The process of big data-based air pollution measurement and urban environmental regeneration for Tehran is implemented based on the following steps. First, from the 22 regions of Tehran, the regions of 2, 5, 9, 10, 21 and 22 were chosen as the case study area which are located in the west and north-west of the city. These regions consist of 25 sub-regions and six air pollution control stations which monitor PM 2.5 pollutants in real time (24 hours/day). Figure 4.5 indicates the case study and analysis area.

In the second step, the average monthly data of PM 2.5 pollutant were extracted from December 2019 to December 2020 and from the AQCC website. The geographical distribution of the extracted data was then estimated through the interpolation model to categorize the pollution level

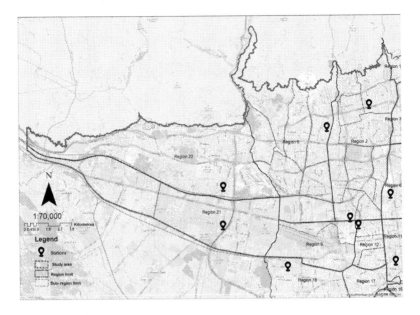

Figure 4.5 The case study and analysis area

in different regions. In the third step, Ordinary Kriging was used as the interpolation model. This technique is a geo-statistical method based on the weighted moving average and calculates the amount of pollutant at a point of the region which is an appropriate model for the spatial zoning of air pollution [67]. Following that, the monthly PM 2.5 concentration data were interpolated into the annual average for model analysis (Figure 4.6).

In addition, since literature suggests that the urban spatial factors including land use, transportation, green space and physical form significantly affect the concentration level of air pollutants, the optimization of these factors was also considered for urban regeneration [7] (Table 4.3).

• Land use.

Urban land use distribution (commercial, official) has a strong relationship with private car uses and residents' commutes and increases the air pollution [68]. Moreover, industrial land use raises the air pollution of the surrounding urban areas [7]. Therefore, commercial, official and industrial land uses were chosen for evaluating their impacts on the air pollution concentrations. It is assumed that these land uses have a direct correlation with the pollution concentration.

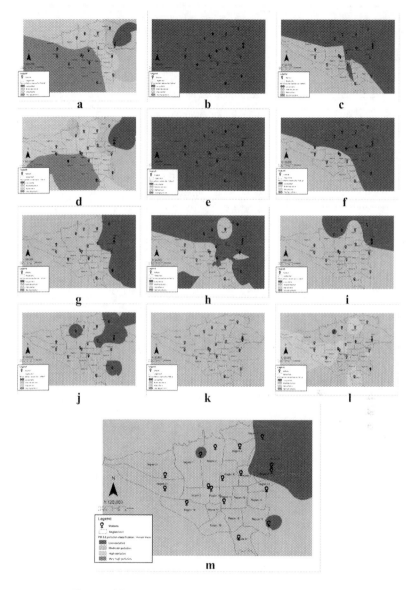

Figure 4.6 The monthly average (a–l) and annual average of PM 2.5 pollutant (m)

Table 4.3 Urban planning factors for GWR analysis and design intervention

Factors	Metrics/types
Urban land use	Commercial, official, industrial
Physical form	Ground Space Index (GSI)
Transportation	Length of roads
Urban vegetation	Parks, green space areas

- Green space.

Urban green spaces have strong and positive effects on air pollution reduction in light of their physical, biological and ecological procedures [69]. Holistically, vegetation can be considered a very useful practice for improving the air quality as pollutants are absorbed through the foliage of trees [70, 71]. Hence, the distribution and the association of parks and green spaces with the air pollution were analyzed based on this assumption that the distribution of green spaces have an inverse relationship with the pollution.

- Physical form.

It is argued that the air circulation greatly diminishes if the urban environment has a dense morphology of buildings. This issue leads to more air pollution concentration in public urban spaces. In other words, the spatial form can affect urban air pollutant dispersion through its influence on the wind flow [72]. Wind flow behaviour is determined through the form and order of buildings. Buildings act as the barriers towards the wind flows in urban areas and, hence, analyzing their density could be significant for the air pollution reduction practices. With this regard, the Ground Space Index (GSI) was chosen as the variable which explains the built environment density. GSI indicates the compactness of an area. It presents what percentage of an area is covered by a building footprint. The higher this index is, the more land is constructed within an area and the area is more compact. In this study, the GSI was analyzed and its relationship with PM 2.5 pollutant was evaluated.

- Transportation.

It is evident that traffic is one of the main sources of air pollution in cities. The traffic congestion raises the fuel consumption and, consequently, affects the ambient air quality [68]. Thus, the length of all road types was chosen for analyzing its correlation with PM 2.5 pollutants.

These urban planning factors set the ground for analysis of the current situation and the effects on the distribution of PM 2.5 in the analysis model (Figure 4.7).

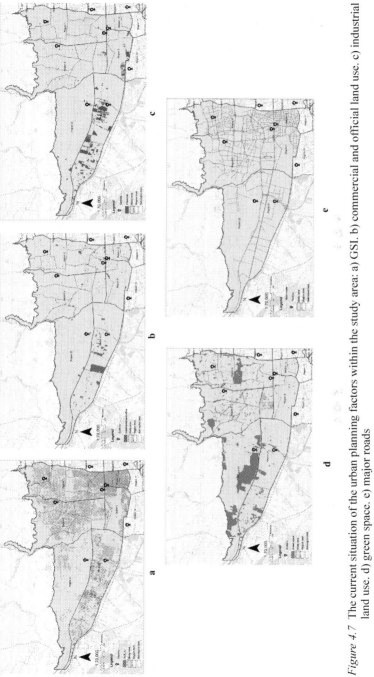

Figure 4.7 The current situation of the urban planning factors within the study area: a) GSI. b) commercial and official land use. c) industrial land use. d) green space. e) major roads

The effects of urban spatial factors on PM 2.5 concentrations were evaluated through the Geographically Weighted Regression (GWR) model. The GWR is a spatial regression model that marks spatially continuous coefficients of all variables over the study area and is widely applied in environmental pollution studies [73]. It assists in analyzing the unstable situation of the spatially varied relationship between independent variables and dependent variables [74]. Holistically, GWR considers spatial heterogeneity and generates discriminated estimations of regression factors across spatial locations [75]. The primary idea of GWR is to detect how the relationship between a dependent variable (Y) and one or more independent variables (X) might geographically vary. According to Fotheringham et al., the GWR is the measurement of the correlation among variables which changes from the one to another location [76].

In this study, the regression model was conducted via the GWR application of the spatial statistics tool in ArcGIS 10.7.1 software. The annual average of PM 2.5 pollutant was chosen as a dependent variable and urban spatial factors (length of roads, GSI, commercial-official area ratio, industrial area ratio and green space area ratio) were set as the independent variables for performing the GWR correlation analysis.

Meanwhile, suitable design principles in four aspects of land use, transportation, physical forms, and urban vegetation were extracted from literature. The critical regions suffering from PM 2.5 were then identified based on the average monthly PM 2.5 concentration maps, and their increasing or decreasing effects were determined through the GWR. Finally, different design principles and intervention strategies were developed. Figure 4.8 presents the process of data analysis.

Data Analysis and Results

GWR was used to determine a set of local regression results including local R2 values. The R2 value ranges from 0 to 1 and the higher value (closer to 1) means that the independent variable can explain more spatial variance of the dependent variable. The lower value of R2 (that is closer to 0) indicates that the independent variable does not have the significant effect and ability to explain the spatial variability in the dependent variable [76]. In this research, the obtained R2 value, after performing GWR analysis, is 0.82 which means that the identified independent variable can explain more spatial variance of the dependent variable. The local coefficient of independent variables was then mapped, and it reveals the influence of independent variables (as the following discussions) in reducing or increasing the air pollution in the study area.

The coefficient of green spaces as an independent variable is predominately negative in the study area and it exactly corresponds to what it is

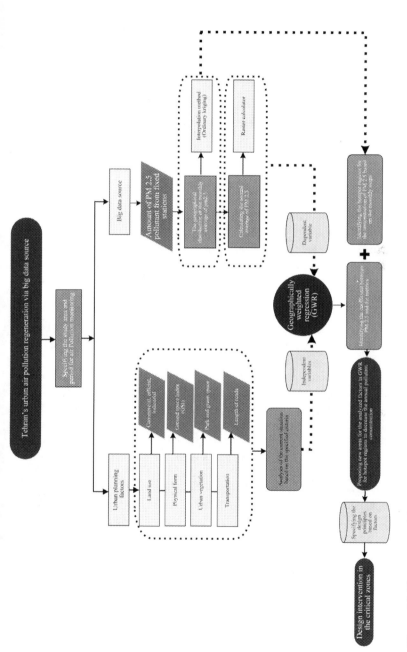

Figure 4.8 The process of data analysis

supposed to be. It means that more green space area leads to a decline in PM 2.5 pollutant. Based on the GWR analysis, the impact of the green space coefficient in Regions 9 and 21, and part of Region 5 are greater than the other regions in decreasing the air pollution. This can be due to the proximity of these areas to higher levels of green space percentage (Figure 4.9).

Likewise, based on the GWR analysis, the coefficient of the GSI as an independent variable is negative in the study area. This finding indicates that if this coefficient increases, it will significantly reduce the PM 2.5 pollutant. In Region 22 and part of the Regions 5 and 21, this factor has the greatest impact on reducing the air pollution in comparison with the other regions. This result is exactly consistent with the project assumptions. These regions are, relatively, the newly built areas of Tehran and their GSI index is lower than the other regions. Therefore, the prevailing wind of Tehran which blows from the west can be more circulated in these regions, with more effective air ventilation because of less construction density (Figure 4.10).

On the other hand, the coefficient of the land use factor for the official and commercial areas as an independent variable is positive in the study area as hypothesized, meaning that this factor has a direct correlation with the PM 2.5 pollutant. It was also identified that this factor is more influential for intensifying the PM 2.5 amount in some parts of Regions 2 and 5, as compared to the other regions. The level of the commercial and official land uses is not that high in these regions; however, this finding could be due to the commercial and official land uses which are located in the surrounding regions (Figure 4.11).

In the same vein, there is a direct correlation between the coefficient of the industrial land use with the amount of the pollutant in most of the study areas. The level of the influence of this factor in some parts of Region 2 is more than the other regions due to the proximity to the larger industrial areas. In addition, this region is surrounded by the Alborz Mountains to its north which functions as an obstacle and escalates the pollution. Region 21 is highly allocated to the industrial area and it is even considered the industrial precinct of Tehran. Therefore, based on the GWR coefficients, its impact on the adjacent regions is observable. This is because of the prevailing wind in Tehran which blows from the west and moves the pollutants to the downtown and north of Tehran. As a result, Regions 9, 10 and 21 are influenced by Region 21 pollution (Figure 4.12).

With reference to the transportation factor, the coefficient of the road length as an independent variable is positive and it has a direct correlation with PM 2.5 pollutant. In Regions 21 and 22, this factor is most effective on the pollution level. These regions are far from the city centre and urban facilities. Consequently, the time required for commuting to the main urban facilities is longer than the other regions and this leads to raise the air pollution in these areas (Figure 4.13).

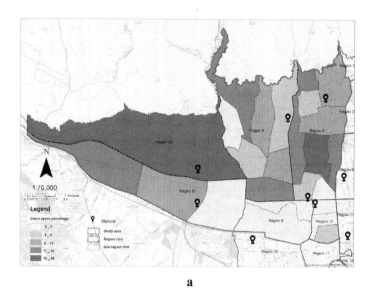

a

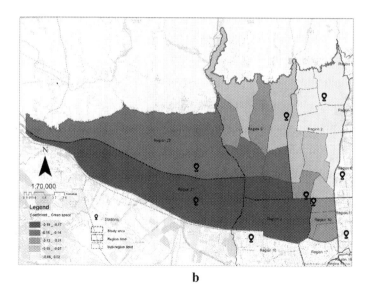

b

Figure 4.9 a) green space percentage in the study area. b) GWR coefficient distribution of green space areas

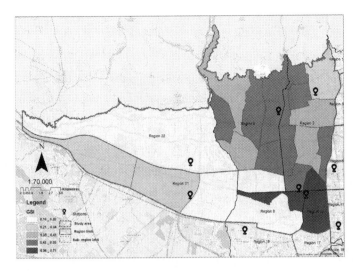

a

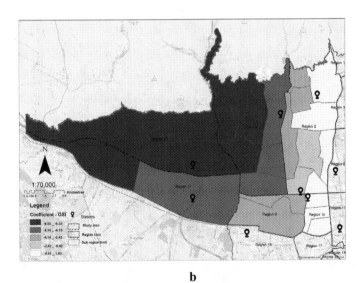

b

Figure 4.10 a) the GSI percentage of the study area. b) the GWR coefficient distribution
of GSI

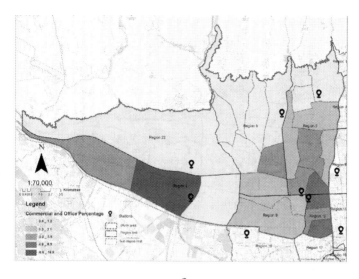

a

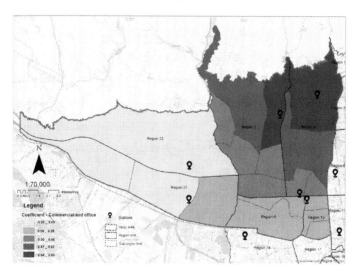

b

Figure 4.11 a) the official and commercial land use percentages in the study area. b)
the GWR coefficient distribution of the land uses

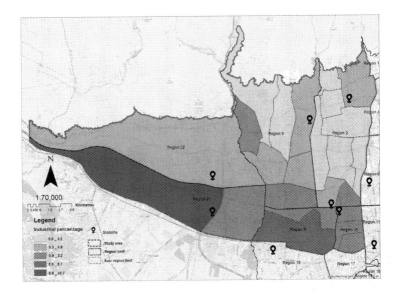

a

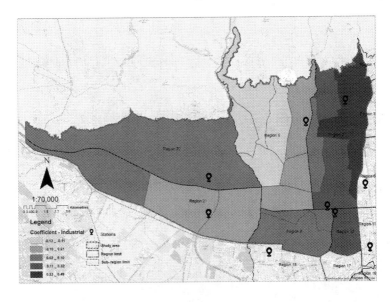

b

Figure 4.12 a) the industrial land use percentage in the study area. b) the GWR coefficient distribution of the industrial land use

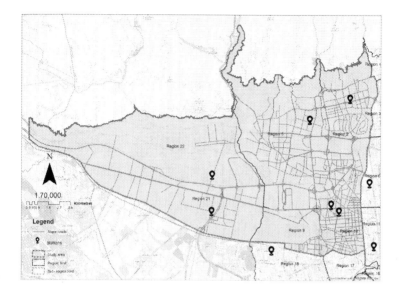

a

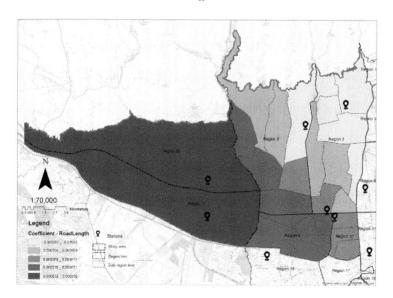

b

Figure 4.13 a) the road lengths in the study area. b) the GWR coefficient distribution
of the road length

Region 10 for the Design Intervention

Based on the monthly average of PM 2.5 pollution in Tehran (Figure 4.7), the regions of the west, south and central parts of Tehran suffer from high pollution in three months of the year. In this interface, Region 10 is identified as one the critical regions of Tehran which suffers from air pollution and very high levels of PM 2.5 pollutant. Therefore, it was chosen as the case study for the regenerative design interventions in this section (Figure 4.14).

According to the GWR analysis, Region 10 is one of the regions in which GSI coefficient has the least impact on reducing the air pollution, compared to the other regions (Table 4.4). The analysis shows that the GSI factor has a high value in this region and the level of construction is, therefore, dense. As a consequence, this region is not ventilated, and the pollutants are trapped. As the design intervention consideration, some open space areas like public spaces can be considered in the brown field grounds to enhance the air circulation and ventilation. Moreover, based on the GWR analysis, it was revealed that the industrial land use has a high level of impact on increasing the air pollution in this region, due to various reasons. First, the industrial land use is allocated to a large area in comparison with the total area of the region. Second, the GSI is higher in this region which leads to stagnation of the industrial pollutants in the region. Third, the industrial

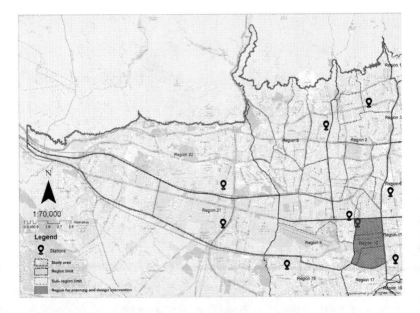

Figure 4.14 Region 10 for the design intervention

pollution of the surrounding regions intensifies the polluting impacts on this area. Hence, the design strategy is proposed to move the industrial land use to the other regions or apply mitigation strategies for decreasing the destructive and consequential impacts on the region.

Commercial and official land use coefficients do not considerably increase the PM 2.5 pollutant in this region; the areas allocated to these land uses are relatively high, though. This finding, hence, leads to a fewer number of travels in these areas because of the better access to urban services for inhabitants. Similarly, the statistical analysis indicates that the green space coefficient has a moderate effect in decreasing the PM 2.5 pollutant. This is because the dedicated areas for the green space land use are relatively low in this region and the surrounding regions lack the sufficient green space area too. Hence, it is proposed to allocate more green space in this region.

As to the transportation factor, the GWR analysis reveals a moderate impact of the road length coefficient on the air pollution increase, compared to the other regions. Nevertheless, the negative impacts of this factor can be mitigated through the design and executive measures mentioned in Table 4.5. Based on the GWR findings, new areas can be ultimately proposed for urban planning factors to decrease the annual average of the air pollution. Progressively, the annual average concentration of PM 2.5 was also analyzed through the linear regression impact of proposing the areas for industrial, commercial and official land uses, green space, GSI and the road length. Applying these changes, the annual average of PM 2.5 concentration can be decreased by 10%.

In a nutshell, based on the GWR analysis and the proposed design principles, Table 4.5 presents the summary and sketch of the regenerative urban design strategies in four aspects of the physical form, land use, transportation and urban vegetation for Region 10. Figure 4.15 also illustrates the strategic and executive plan of regeneration for these aspects in the studied region.

• Land use.

It is proposed to transfer the industrial land use to other regions and use their space, in turn, as a public space. The accessibility to neighbourhood services should be also considered to decrease unnecessary travel of residents to other regions for procuring their daily requirements.

• Vegetation.

Green spaces, continuous green lines, green roofs and green walls are proposed for improving the quality of air. In Region B, there is an open space which is allocated to public parking in the current situation, but we propose the transformation of this function to green space and having green walls combined (Figures 4.16–4.20). In Region A, the open space among

Table 4.4 Proposed areas of urban planning factors for air pollution reduction in Region 10

Urban planning factors	Region 10	Coefficient	Intercept	Residual	Existing area	Existing annually average of PM 2.5 concentration	Proposed area	Proposed annual average of PM 2.5 concentration
Industrial	Sub-region 1	0.28	29.92	0.9	1.13%	32.59	0.2%	29.93
Commercial		0.20			5.46%		7%	
Road length		0.0000146			22975		20000	
Green space		–0.12			3.78%		25%	
Ground Spaces Index		0.74			0.64%		0.5%	
Industrial	Sub-region 2	0.27	29.92	0.76	1.44%	32.51	0.1%	30.08
Commercial		0.23			3.5%		5%	
Road length		0.0000143			27200		26000	
Green space		–0.12			0.34%		20%	
Ground Spaces Index		0.35			0.68%		0.5%	
Industrial	Sub-region 3	0.31	29.47	0.26	1.62%	32.16	0.2%	30.04
Commercial		0.29			4.76%		6%	
Road length		0.0000105			25568		24000	
Green space		–0.10			0.79%		20%	
Ground Space Index		0.52			0.64%		0.5%	

Existing annual average PM 2.5 concentration in Region 10 32.42

Proposed annual average PM 2.5 concentration for Region 10 30.01

Table 4.5 Regenerative urban design principles for reducing air pollution in Region 10

Factor	Regenerative design strategies	Reference	Sketch
Physical form	Considering porosity and open space in urban blocks to diminish building density and increase air circulation	[77–80]	
	Eliminating the ground floor for passing the air	[77, 81]	
	Channelling the street canyons	[77, 82, 83]	
	Omitting the corners	[77]	

(Continued)

Table 4.5 (Continued)

Factor	Regenerative design strategies	Reference	Sketch
	Creating public spaces in urban areas	[84]	
	Creating variation in building heights such as stepped variation	[78, 80, 81]	
	Locating the long side of a high-rise building parallel or within a 30° angle to the dominant wind direction	[78]	
	Making porosity in buildings	[81]	

Land use		
Development of the compact mixed land use including residential, shopping facilities, sport complex, schools, restaurants and public spaces	[84–86]	
Providing urban facilities in walkable distance	[85]	
Locating industries downwind to avoid pollutant flow toward residential areas	[87]	
Using green space as an obstacle between industrial and residential areas	[87]	

(Continued)

Table 4.5 (Continued)

Factor	Regenerative design strategies	Reference	Sketch
Transportation	Changing the position of parking spaces	[77]	
	Blocking streets to cars and developing walkability	[77, 84, 88]	
	Providing pedestrian and bicycle access to stations and between building blocks	[85, 89]	
	Providing routes for all modes of transportation	[85]	

	Distributing traffic between parallel streets instead of collecting them in some roads	[85]	
	Decreasing the distances between places to reduce trip times	[85]	
Urban vegetation	Suggesting green intersections	[77]	
	Proposing green roofs, green surfaces and green walls as a furniture in public spaces	[77, 81, 90]	

(Continued)

Table 4.5 (Continued)

Factor	Regenerative design strategies	Reference	Sketch
	Planting trees along the line (downwind) and one line (in middle) of streets	[77]	
	Creating continuity of the urban green space (the combination of artificial green spaces with natural spaces)	[78]	
	Using evergreen species	[90, 91]	
	Implementing large-scale urban ventilation corridors and green belts in urban areas	[78, 85]	

Green space in walkable places, sidewalks, public spaces and semi-public spaces	[77, 88, 92]	
Using shrub species and trees with a spread canopy, instead of dense canopy trees, to prevent air stagnation in street canyons and high shrubs close to open roadside areas	[91]	

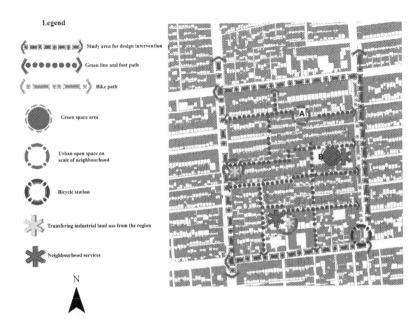

Figure 4.15 Regenerative strategic plan for PM 2.5 reduction in the region

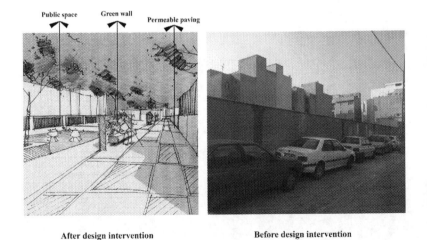

Figure 4.16 Physical actions (positioning the green wall and permeable paving) to decrease air pollution in Region B

After design intervention   **Before design intervention**

Figure 4.17 Prioritizing the green transportation (priority to pedestrians and eliminate marginal parking) in Region B

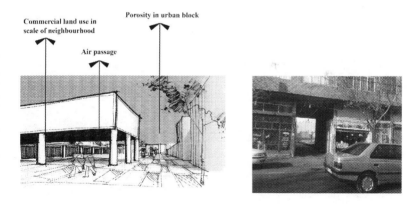

After design intervention   **Before design intervention**

Figure 4.18 Changing the public parking to green space area in Region B

buildings, which is the place for car parks, is proposed to be converted into public space including green spaces and trees (Figure 4.21).

•   Transportation.

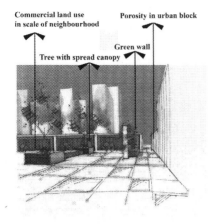

After design intervention　　　　　　**Before design intervention**

Figure 4.19　Physical and functional changes in Region B

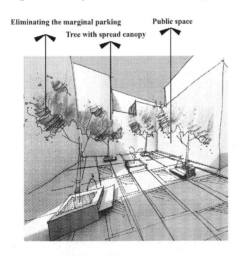

After design intervention　　　　　　**Before design intervention**

Figure 4.20　Creating urban open space for pedestrians in Region B

　　Continuous walking paths, cycling lines and bicycle stations are proposed to be included in the region and decrease the dependence of inhabitants on private cars.

- Physical form.

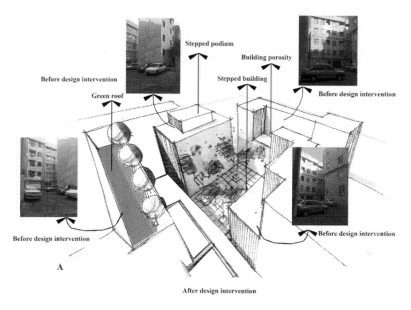

Figure 4.21 Physical design interventions (building porosity, stepped building, green roof, stepped podium) to Region A

Due to the higher GSI in the region, it is proposed to alleviate this problem with changing the height of buildings and creating more porosity in buildings and urban blocks.

Conclusion

It can be concluded that big data sources are a reliable basis for environmental planning, urban sustainability regeneration and urban design interventions. With the explained processes for discovering relationships between the amounts and patterns of pollutants, obtained through real-time sources and big data technologies, it is technically feasible to perform planning for urban environments and design urban areas in the ways which mitigate the destructive impacts of air pollution. Moreover, social and economic sustainability can be achieved on top of environmental sustainability, through creating proper public spaces, open spaces, green spaces and urban services and amenities for impacted urban precincts.

Note

1 PM 2.5 refers to the fine particles of dust smaller than 2.5 μm diameter and is the indicator that the World Health Organization (WHO) applies to evaluate the air pollution because of its direct correlation with serious health impacts.

References

1 Saaty, T.L. and P. De Paola, Rethinking design and urban planning for the cities of the future. *Buildings*, 2017. **7**(3): p. 76.

2 Hswen, Y., et al., Feasibility of using social media to monitor outdoor air pollution in London, England. *Preventive Medicine*, 2019. **121**: p. 86–93.

3 Marjanović, M., S. Grubeša, and I.P. Žarko. Air and noise pollution monitoring in the city of Zagreb by using mobile crowdsensing. In *2017 25th International Conference on Software, Telecommunications and Computer Networks (SoftCOM)*. 2017. IEEE.

4 Maisonneuve, N., M. Stevens, and B. Ochab, Participatory noise pollution monitoring using mobile phones. *Information Polity*, 2010. **15**(1, 2): p. 51–71.

5 Wu, J. and I.-S. Chang, Environmental planning. In *Environmental Management in China*. 2020, Springer. p. 17–34.

6 Brambilla, G. and F. Pedrielli, Smartphone-based participatory soundscape mapping for a more sustainable acoustic environment. *Sustainability*, 2020. **12**(19): p. 7899.

7 Guo, L., et al., The influence of urban planning factors on PM2.5 pollution exposure and implications: A case study in China based on remote sensing, LBS, and GIS data. *Science of the Total Environment*, 2019. **659**: p. 1585–1596.

8 Jiang, W., et al., Using social media to detect outdoor air pollution and monitor Air Quality Index (AQI): A geo-targeted spatiotemporal analysis framework with Sina Weibo (Chinese Twitter). *PloS One*, 2015. **10**(10): p. e0141185.

9 Roseline, R., M. Devapriya, and P. Sumathi, Pollution monitoring using sensors and wireless sensor networks: A survey. *International Journal of Application or Innovation in Engineering & Management*, 2013. **2**(7): p. 119–124.

10 Shi, Y. and H. Gao, *Using social media for air pollution detection-the case of Eastern China smog*. 2017.

11 Kay, S., B. Zhao, and D. Sui, Can social media clear the air? A case study of the air pollution problem in Chinese cities. *The Professional Geographer*, 2015. **67**(3): p. 351–363.

12 Mei, S., et al. Inferring air pollution by sniffing social media. In *2014 IEEE/ACM International Conference on Advances in Social Networks Analysis and Mining (ASONAM 2014)*. 2014. IEEE.

13 Kasar, A.R., D.S. Khemnar, and N.P. Tembhurnikar, WSN based air pollution monitoring system. *International Journal of Science and Engineering Applications*, 2013. **2**(4): p. 55–59.

14 Hu, K., et al. SVR based dense air pollution estimation model using static and wireless sensor network. In *2016 IEEE SENSORS*. 2016. IEEE.

15 Yi, W.Y., et al., A survey of wireless sensor network based air pollution monitoring systems. *Sensors*, 2015. **15**(12): p. 31392–31427.

16 Boubrima, A., W. Bechkit, and H. Rivano, Optimal WSN deployment models for air pollution monitoring. *IEEE Transactions on Wireless Communications*, 2017. **16**(5): p. 2723–2735.

17 Liu, J.-H., et al., An air quality monitoring system for urban areas based on the technology of wireless sensor networks. *International Journal on Smart Sensing & Intelligent Systems*, 2012. **5**(1).

18 Khedo, K.K., R. Perseedoss, and A. Mungur, A wireless sensor network air pollution monitoring system. *arXiv preprint arXiv:1005.1737*, 2010.
19 Mansour, S., et al. Wireless sensor network-based air quality monitoring system. In *2014 International Conference on Computing, Networking and Communications (ICNC)*. 2014. IEEE.
20 Jamil, M.S., et al., Smart environment monitoring system by employing wireless sensor networks on vehicles for pollution free smart cities. *Procedia Engineering*, 2015. **107**: p. 480–484.
21 Raju, P.V., R. Aravind, and B.S. Kumar, Pollution monitoring system using wireless sensor network in Visakhapatnam. *International Journal of Engineering Trends and Technology*, 2013. **4**(4): p. 591–595.
22 Tajne, K., S. Rathore, and G. Asutkar, Monitoring of air pollution using wireless sensors: A case study of monitoring air pollution in Nagpur city. *International Journal of Environmental Sciences*, 2011. **2**(2): p. 829–838.
23 Mujawar, T., V. Bachuwar, and S. Suryavanshi, Air pollution monitoring system in Solapur city using wireless sensor network. *Proceedings Published by International Journal of Computer Applications®(IJCA), CCSN-2013 (1)*, 2013: p. 11–15.
24 Fotue, D., G.-A. Tanonkou, and T. Engel. An ad-hoc wireless sensor networks with application to air pollution detection. In *SNA*. 2009.
25 Kadri, A., et al. Wireless sensor network for real-time air pollution monitoring. In *2013 1st International Conference on Communications, Signal Processing, and Their Applications (ICCSPA)*. 2013. IEEE.
26 Boubrima, A., et al. Optimal deployment of wireless sensor networks for air pollution monitoring. In *2015 24th International Conference on Computer Communication and Networks (ICCCN)*. 2015. IEEE.
27 Swagarya, G., S. Kaijage, and R.S. Sinde, A survey on wireless sensor networks application for air pollution monitoring. *International Journal of Engineering and Computer Science*, 2014. **3**(5): p. 5975–5979.
28 Hejlová, V. and V. Voženílek, Wireless sensor network components for air pollution monitoring in the urban environment: Criteria and analysis for their selection. *Wireless Sensor Network*, 2013. **5**(12): p. 229.
29 Sammarco, M., et al., Using geosocial search for urban air pollution monitoring. *Pervasive and Mobile Computing*, 2017. **35**: p. 15–31.
30 Jiang, W., et al., Using geo-targeted social media data to detect outdoor air pollution. *The International Archives of Photogrammetry, Remote Sensing and Spatial Information Sciences*, 2016. **41**: p. 553.
31 Sha, Y., J. Yan, and G. Cai. Detecting public sentiment over PM2.5 pollution hazards through analysis of Chinese microblog. In *ISCRAM*. 2014.
32 Zuo, J., et al., Mapping urban environmental noise using smartphones. *Sensors*, 2016. **16**(10): p. 1692.
33 Maisonneuve, N., et al., NoiseTube: Measuring and mapping noise pollution with mobile phones. In *Information Technologies in Environmental Engineering*. 2009, Springer. p. 215–228.
34 D'Hondt, E., M. Stevens, and A. Jacobs, Participatory noise mapping works! An evaluation of participatory sensing as an alternative to standard techniques for environmental monitoring. *Pervasive and Mobile Computing*, 2013. **9**(5): p. 681–694.

35 Kanjo, E., Noisespy: A real-time mobile phone platform for urban noise monitoring and mapping. *Mobile Networks and Applications*, 2010. **15**(4): p. 562–574.
36 Kardous, C.A. and P.B. Shaw, Evaluation of smartphone sound measurement applications. *The Journal of the Acoustical Society of America*, 2014. **135**(4): p. EL186–EL192.
37 Liu, T., et al., Methods for sensing urban noises. *Technical Report MSR-TR-2014-66*, 2014.
38 Hara, S., et al. Sound sensing using smartphones as a crowdsourcing approach. In *2017 Asia-Pacific Signal and Information Processing Association Annual Summit and Conference (APSIPA ASC)*. 2017. IEEE.
39 Stevens, M. and E. D'Hondt. Crowdsourcing of pollution data using smartphones. In *Workshop on Ubiquitous Crowdsourcing*. 2010.
40 Zamora Mero, W.J., *Crowdsensing solutions for urban pollution monitoring using smartphones*. 2019.
41 Maisonneuve, N., M. Stevens, and L. Steels, *Measure and map noise pollution with your mobile phone*. 2009.
42 Nouri, A., et al., Evaluation of noise pollution in Parks of Sanandaj City and zoning with geographic information system. *Journal of Advances in Environmental Health Research*, 2016. **4**(4): p. 206–212.
43 Gubbi, J., et al. A pilot study of urban noise monitoring architecture using wireless sensor networks. In *2013 International Conference on Advances in Computing, Communications and Informatics (ICACCI)*. 2013. IEEE.
44 Mariscal-Ramirez, J., et al. Knowledge-based wireless sensors using sound pressure level for noise pollution monitoring. In *2011 11th International Conference on Intelligent Systems Design and Applications*. 2011. IEEE.
45 Peckens, C., C. Porter, and T. Rink, Wireless sensor networks for long-term monitoring of urban noise. *Sensors*, 2018. **18**(9): p. 3161.
46 Aggarwal, S., S. Kumar, and K.K. Ahirwar. Architecture: Noise pollution monitor through wireless sensor network. In *Conference Proceedings-SEEK DIGITAL LIBRARY*. 2011.
47 Alías, F. and R.M. Alsina-Pagès, Review of wireless acoustic sensor networks for environmental noise monitoring in smart cities. *Journal of Sensors*, 2019. **2019**.
48 Filipponi, L., S. Santini, and A. Vitaletti. Data collection in wireless sensor networks for noise pollution monitoring. In *International Conference on Distributed Computing in Sensor Systems*. 2008. Springer.
49 Santini, S., B. Ostermaier, and A. Vitaletti. First experiences using wireless sensor networks for noise pollution monitoring. In *Proceedings of the Workshop on Real-World Wireless Sensor Networks*. 2008.
50 Cantuna, J.G., S. Solórzano, and J.-M. Clairand. Noise pollution measurement system using wireless sensor network and BAN sensors. In *2017 Fourth International Conference on eDemocracy & eGovernment (ICEDEG)*. 2017. IEEE.
51 Singla, T. and M.S. Manshahia, *Wireless sensor networks for pollution monitoring and control*. 2017.
52 Kivelä, I. and I. Hakala. Area-based environmental noise measurements with a wireless sensor network. In *Proceedings of the Euronoise*. 2015.

53 Segura-Garcia, J., et al., Low-cost alternatives for urban noise nuisance monitoring using wireless sensor networks. *IEEE Sensors Journal*, 2014. **15**(2): p. 836–844.

54 Masroor, K., et al., Spatial modelling of PM2.5 concentrations in Tehran using Kriging and inverse distance weighting (IDW) methods. *Journal of Air Pollution and Health*, 2020. **5**(2): p. 89–96.

55 Abbasi, M., M.H. Hosseinlou, and S. Jafarzadeh Fadaki, An investigation of Bus Rapid Transit System (BRT) based on economic and air pollution analysis (Tehran, Iran). *Case Studies on Transport Policy*, 2020. **8**(2): p. 553–563.

56 Heger, M. and M. Sarraf, *Air pollution in Tehran: Health costs, sources, and policies*. 2018. World Bank.

57 Mohammadi-Zadeh, M.J., et al., An analysis of air pollutants' emission coefficient in the transport sector of Tehran. *Open Journal of Ecology*, 2017. **7**(05): p. 309.

58 Torbatian, S., et al., Air pollution trends in Tehran and their anthropogenic drivers. *Atmospheric Pollution Research*, 2020. **11**(3): p. 429–442.

59 Asadollah-Fardi, G.J.A.o.J., Air quality management in Tehran. 2008. **19**.

60 Asadollah-Fardi, G. Current situation of air pollution in Tehran with emphasis on district 12. In *First Kitakyushu Initiative Meeting, Kitakyushu, Japan*. 2001.

61 Jafarian, H. and S.J.P. Behzadi, Evaluation of PM2.5 emissions in Tehran by means of remote sensing and regression models. *Environmental Science*, 2020. **6**(3): p. 521–529.

62 Motesaddi, S., Y. Hashempour, and P.J.C.E.J. Nowrouz, Characterizing of air pollution in Tehran: Comparison of two air quality indices. *Civil Engineering Journal*, 2017. **3**(9): p. 749–758.

63 Faridi, S., et al., Long-term trends and health impact of PM2.5 and O3 in Tehran, Iran, 2006–2015. *Environment International*, 2018. **114**: p. 37–49.

64 Moshfeghi, V., N.G. Haghighat, and M. Habibi, *Land use and the efficiency of transportation laws with regard to air pollution in Tehran metropolitan area*. 2020.

65 Arhami, M., et al., Seasonal trends in the composition and sources of PM2.5 and carbonaceous aerosol in Tehran, Iran. *Environmental Pollution*, 2018. **239**: p. 69–81.

66 Shahbazi, H., et al., Investigating the influence of traffic emission reduction plans on Tehran air quality using WRF/CAMx modeling tools. *Transportation Research Part D: Transport and Environment*, 2017. **57**: p. 484–495.

67 Birjandi, N., M. Ghobadi, and M. Ahmadi, Analysis and zoning of air pollution in urban landscape using different models of spatial analysis (case study: Tehran). *Advances in Environmental Technology*, 2019. **5**(3): p. 185–191.

68 Vietti, M., *Cleaning the air: Mitigating air pollution through urban design*. Master Thesis, TU Delft Architecture and the Built Environment; TU Delft Urbanism. 2017.

69 Mori, J., F. Ferrini, and A. Saebo, Air pollution mitigation by urban greening. *Italus Hortus*, 2018. **25**: p. 13–22.

70 Cho, H.-S. and M.J. Choi, Effects of compact urban development on air pollution: Empirical evidence from Korea. *Sustainability*, 2014. **6**(9): p. 5968–5982.

71 Barwise, Y. and P. Kumar, Designing vegetation barriers for urban air pollution abatement: A practical review for appropriate plant species selection. *npj Climate and Atmospheric Science*, 2020. **3**(1): p. 1–19.

72 Yang, J., et al., Air pollution dispersal in high density urban areas: Research on the triadic relation of wind, air pollution, and urban form. *Sustainable Cities and Society*, 2020. **54**: p. 101941.

73 Zhou, Q., C. Wang, and S. Fang, Application of geographically weighted regression (GWR) in the analysis of the cause of haze pollution in China. *Atmospheric Pollution Research*, 2019. **10**(3): p. 835–846.

74 Jiang, M., et al., Modelling seasonal GWR of daily PM2.5 with proper auxiliary variables for the Yangtze River Delta. *Remote Sensing*, 2017. **9**(4): p. 346.

75 Li, S., et al., Spatial heterogeneity in the determinants of urban form: An analysis of Chinese cities with a GWR approach. *Sustainability*, 2019. **11**(2): p. 479.

76 Daful, M., et al., Assessment of the spatial relationship between air pollutants in Kaduna Metropolis, Nigeria. *Journal of Sustainable Development*, 2020. **13**(4).

77 Yang, J., et al., Air pollution dispersal in high density urban areas: Research on the triadic relation of wind, air pollution, and urban form. *Sustainable Cities and Society*, 2020. **54**: p. 101941.

78 Cho, H.-S. and M.J. Choi, Effects of compact urban development on air pollution: Empirical evidence from Korea. *Sustainability*, 2014. **6**(9): p. 5968–5982.

79 Yang, J., et al., Urban form and air pollution disperse: Key indexes and mitigation strategies. *Sustainable Cities and Society*, 2020. **57**: p. 101955.

80 Hu, H., *Breathing city: Mitigating air pollution through urban microclimate design.* Master thesis, (TU Delft Architecture and the Built Environment) , Delft University of Technology, 2020.

81 Theurer, W., Typical building arrangements for urban air pollution modelling. *Atmospheric Environment*, 1999. **33**(24–25): p. 4057–4066.

82 Sadat Sadrolgharavi, T. and M.J. Mahdavinejad, The form of residential buildings on local winds: Air pollution reduction. *International Journal of Architecture and Urban Development*, 2018. **8**(1): p. 53–64.

83 Karlson 'Charlie' Hargroves, D.C., L. Gallina, and P. Newman, *Sustainable urban design co-benefits*. Intergovernmental Eleventh Regional Environmentally Sustainable Transport (EST) Forum in Asia, 2–5 October 2018, Ulaanbaatar, Mongolia.

84 Gupta P.R. Reduction in Urban Air Pollution During COVID–19 Lockdown Can Be Control by Implementation of Sustainable Urban Planning Strategies. *IRE J*, 2020 Jul. 4: 99–108.

85 Wachs, M., Learning from Los Angeles: transport, urban form, and air quality. *Transportation*, 1993. **20**(4): p. 329–354.

86 Rydell, C.P. and G. Schwarz, Air pollution and urban form: A review of current literature. *Journal of the American Institute of Planners*, 1968. **34**(2): p. 115–120.

87 Shafray, E. and S. Kim, A study of walkable spaces with natural elements for urban regeneration: A focus on cases in Seoul, South Korea. *Sustainability*, 2017. **9**(4): p. 587.

88 Vardoulakis, S., et al., Local action on outdoor air pollution to improve public health. *International Journal of Public Health*, 2018. **63**(5): p. 557–565.
89 Anamika, A. and C. Pradeep, Urban vegetation and air pollution mitigation: Some issues from India. *Chinese Journal of Urban and Environmental Studies*, 2016. **4**(01): p. 1650001.
90 Mori, J., F. Ferrini, and A. Saebo, Air pollution mitigation by urban greening. *Italus Hortus*, 2018. **25**: p. 13–22.
91 Barwise, Y. and P. Kumar, Designing vegetation barriers for urban air pollution abatement: A practical review for appropriate plant species selection. *npj Climate and Atmospheric Science*, 2020. **3**(1): p. 1–19.

5   Big Data and Urban Social Sustainability

Social Sustainability in Urban Planning and Design

Social sustainability is usually argued as being an essential element of urban sustainability, which has increased in awareness recently [1]. It is delineated as a mechanism ensuring the well-being of the current and future generations and the satisfaction of humans' primary requirements, strongly correlated to improving the quality of life, diminishing the social inequalities [2–4] and leading to the community stability [5].

In the urban regeneration context, social sustainability is a procedure for making sustainable, successful places that improve residents' well-being, by perceiving what people expect from the places in which they live and work. It merges the design of the physical domain with the design of social structures to support social and cultural life, social amenities, systems for citizens' participation and space for people to evolve [5].

It is stated that physical and non-physical factors effect on social sustainability of urban communities. The effective physical factors include urbanity, attractive and well-designed public spaces, decent housing, amenities and facilities, accessibility (for example to local services, facilities, employment, green spaces), walkability in neighbourhoods and pedestrian friendliness. Besides, health protection, quality of life and well-being, social inclusion, sense of safety and security, mixed tenure, social cohesion, social participation, sense of place and sense of community, social interaction, vitality and vibrancy of urban spaces are considered as non-physical factors which greatly influence the urban social regeneration [3].

Therefore, residents play a key role in the urban social sustainability and having big data technology makes it feasible to monitor human behaviour in real time and identify the engaged social sustainability agenda. In this chapter, the factors of public space in urban areas, walkability in neighbourhoods, vitality and vibrancy as a quality of spaces were chosen to discuss together with big data technology applications (Figure 5.1).

DOI: 10.4324/9781003139942-5

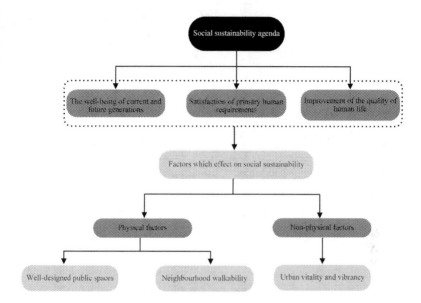

Figure 5.1 The analyzed social sustainability agenda in this chapter

Walkability and Big Data

Walkability was suggested in the late 1990's in the United States as the concept of relating the built environment dimensions to pedestrian traffic [6]. Walking is the most prevalent and available physical form of activity, is environmental friendly and an economical type of physical activity, and walkability points to how friendly an urban area is for pedestrians [7]. The factors effecting walkability are the connectivity of pedestrian infrastructures, characters of pedestrian streetscapes and the perception of safety [8].

Walking, in fact, plays a vital role in developing healthy communities, enhancing economic opportunities and reinforcing social connections [7]. Creating low-carbon, climate-resilient and high well-being communities; diminishing the CO2 and NO emissions; and improving interpersonal communications are among the positive outcomes of improving the urban walkability [9].

It also appears as a fundamental concern for designers and planners of the built environment since it is required to measure the walkability rate [8] and develop an appropriate and quality walking environment as a substantial part of a sustainable city. Urban big data has provided novel opportunities in designing the walkable cities to detect and create in an intelligent approach

[10]. With this respect, big data-driven urban space walkability measurement methods can be consistently applied to measure the street walking spaces on a city scale at a point of time and replace the deficient and inadequate sample sizes and inconsistent scale of manual evaluations [6].

Walkability and GPS Trajectories

The plethora and ubiquity of collected GPS location points (e.g., latitudes and longitudes), are provided through mobile phones equipped with GPS sensors, GPS-enabled watches and/or wrist bands. These technologies have, hence, generated considerable strengths in tracking moving objects data to obtain hotspot regions and identify pedestrians' mobility patterns [11].

The walkability evaluation via the GPS data starts with collecting pedestrian behaviours through mobile GPS tools during the specified time and defined area. Invalid data are eliminated and the features such as location (longitude, latitude), velocity and time are extracted to measure the walkability between other modes of transportation [12]. For specifying the pedestrian flow between other modes of transportation such as bicycles, cars, trains, two criteria should be considered to filter out irrelevant data. First, the average moving speed between two locations for walking and running should be within the threshold values from 6 km/h to 25 km/h. Second, one or more of the two consecutive GPS track points should be positioned between 50 m to 1 km distance. Machine learning algorithms such as classification and clustering applications are also used to distinguish the walk from other modes of transportation.

Next to the filtering and clustering tasks, the spatial distribution of pedestrian densities within different time periods is illustrated through map matching algorithms attaching each GPS track to road segments and the temporal variations of pedestrian numbers are calculated for weekdays and holidays [9, 13]. Based on the number of users and frequencies of activities, it is then applicable to conclude whether a road segment is appropriate for walkability or not [13]. Some indicators are defined to measure which factors influence on walkability and pedestrian flows. This analysis can be done through regression analysis such as GWR to investigate the relationship between influencing factors on walkability [9]. The challenges in using this type of big data for measuring the pedestrian behaviour are the privacy, inaccuracy, inconsistency and scarcity of available data and computational power [10]. On the other hand, it is a cost effective method for collecting a large amount of location data about walking behaviour [14] and pedestrian networks can be effectively identified through its trajectories analysis.

It can be concluded that GPS is functional in finding out pedestrian streams and hotspot regions and measuring the popularity of urban roads for walkability. Moreover, the influential factors on walking behaviour can be identified and analyzed, improving the quality of paving lines to enhance the social communication in urban spaces. Therefore, this can be stated that through the procedure of selection, filter, combination and transformation of GPS datasets, we can create awareness and intelligence towards designing better and more impressive walkable city solutions (Figure 5.2).

Urban Public Space and Big Data

Urban public spaces are effective components of urban structures which boost physical activities, improve mental health and social strength, and deliver economic and ecological values to local communities [15]. Social, cultural and recreational activities are carried out in urban public spaces and therefore, the experience and routine of residents' use of public spaces provide significant information sources for the regeneration. However, conventional approaches (surveys, interviews) are costly and time-consuming and do not reflect the real-time interactions and changes in urban public spaces [16]. With this respect, social media can be applied to monitor and track the human behaviour in urban public spaces in a timely manner.

Urban Public Space and Social Media Data

Social media data as location-based service data like Foursquare, Twitter and Google Places can reflect preferences, use and activities of people in urban public spaces [17]. These platforms deliver comprehensive understanding of the public life because they have high volumes of information and tremendous speeds [15].

The process of social media applications for detecting peoples' behaviour, sentiments and their experience in urban public space commences with extracting the data from the platforms such as Twitter, Foursquare and Google Places during a specified time and from a specified region. The extracted features for analysis usually include time, location, text (geolocated venues with semantic information) and the number of check-ins. Each type of the social media platforms has a particular data archetype. For example, Google Places delivers quantity and types of economic activities, Foursquare datasets include venue quantity and types of demand and Twitter data include spatiotemporal patterns of human activities [17].

The collected data are then pre-processed and analyzed through the following methods:

1) Content analysis which concentrates on eliciting information from texts using natural language processing or text mining topic modelling and word frequency analysis,

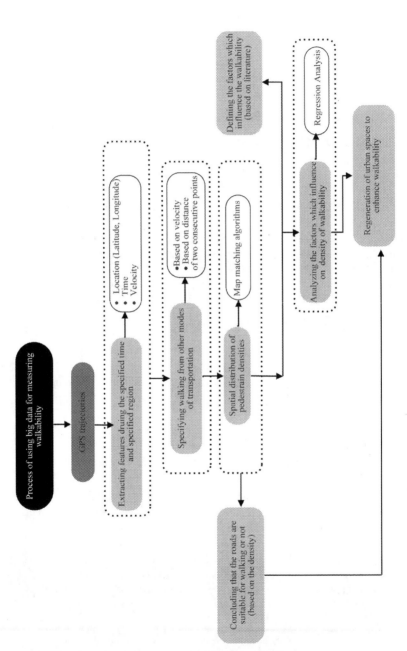

Figure 5.2 Process of using GPS trajectories for measuring walkability

2) Network analysis which detects appropriate information through net-work structures and visualization,

3) Spatial sentiment analysis which figures out peoples' perceptions of social interactions and emotional responses to public spaces through lexicon-based sentiment analysis, GIS spatial analysis and the geo-coded social media data.

In fact, creating a connection between social media sentiment and geo-location data is one of the significant steps to realizing peoples' spatiotem-poral experiences and their viewpoints towards public spaces [16]. Having this type of analysis complete, the data are then classified and visualized through the cartography method [17] and the characteristics, quality and popularity of public spaces are discovered.

There are the advantages in using social media for identifying human behaviour in the urban public spaces:

•   These types of data are convenient and quick to run, inexpensive and easily achievable for designers to understand users' behaviour in public spaces and provide a vision of peoples' use of urban spaces, compared to surveys or interviews [16, 17],

•   Residents' experiences, emotions and preferences on space utilizations and place identity can be specified, and predictive correlations between human movements patterns and their socio-behavioural experiences can be constructed [16],

•   Environmental quality analysis and improvements are conducted by perceiving people's behaviour and interactions with the environment and with the space-time dimension [16],

•   Tourists and people who do not know a city become aware of public spaces and reference points [18],

•   Less tangible aspects and immaterial factors of urban public spaces can be recognized through social media data analysis including socio-spatial subjects [17, 19],

•   Popular public spaces can be recognized through analyzing the fre-quency of visits and viewpoints or preferences of social networks users [18],

•   Quality of urban public spaces including density, diversity, design and potential for regeneration can be measured [19].

On the other hand, social media data are not collected through systematic and statistical methods because they are inherently messy. Fake accounts, missing data and weak categorizations are prevalent problems [15] as well. Furthermore, geo-tagged social media may not that be as precise as GPS-level precision and consequently, location information may not be correct [16].

It can be summarized that social media provides the public-oriented data source which reveals residents' activities, perceptions, preferences and sensations towards urban spaces. This function facilitates the urban spaces quality improvement based on identifying people's demands and priorities (Figure 5.3).

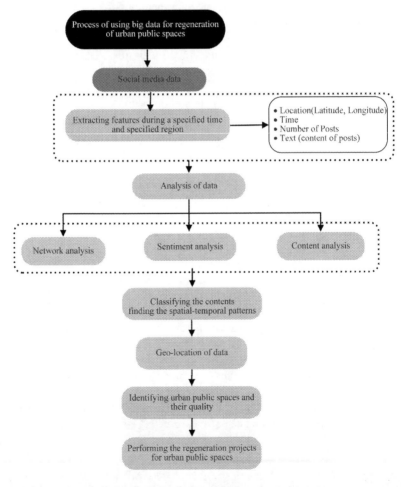

Figure 5.3 Process of applying social media for urban public spaces

Urban Vibrancy and Big Data

There is an increased awareness that creating and maintaining urban vibrancy are fundamental to achieving social and economic sustainability. In fact, the vibrancy develops human activities and interactions, and improves residents' feelings about urban spaces which, in turn, enhances their well-being and innovation capabilities [20]. The idea of urban vibrancy comes from Jacobs' book published in 1961, *The Death and Life of Great American Cities*. It, actually, portrays the attraction, diversity and prosperity of urban spaces emanating from human activities and interactions. Vibrant urban spaces, thus, simplify social communications and interactions and deliver sustainable urbanization in the long run [21].

Vibrancy points out the number of people in and around active or lively areas at different times of the days and nights. This virtue has an impressive effect on the economy and social lives and can result from adequate urban activities, well-designed urban forms and well-developed functions.

In the recent decade, it has become feasible to explore and depict the dynamism of urban vibrancy in a citywide and in fine spatiotemporal scales by applying spatial big data through the quantitative measurements. These types of data can capture the fast-changing urban dynamics in a large sample size (wide spatial coverage) and develop them within a quick update rate, with temporal details and high penetration [20–23]. It is, therefore, to portray and quantify urban vibrancy more conveniently and precisely by such datasets [22].

The Role of Social Media Data in Analyzing Urban Vibrancy

Urban vibrancy is a subjective concept which is difficult to be quantified as there are various factors involved. The intensity of social and economic activities, the land use configurations and functional mixing, pedestrian intensity, accessibility, diversity, community quality, demographic and built environment factors, employment rates, population census data and housing prices effect urban vibrancy [20, 21, 23, 24].

Social media check-in data, such as Facebook, Twitter, Sina Weibo, as spatial and temporal data are useful to characterize the vibrancy of a city [24]. These types of data can measure the urban vibrancy with capturing the intensity of social and spatial economic activities and identifying the spatial structure and distributions [20]. Accordingly, location (latitude and longitude) and time are substantial factors indicating the patterns of social and economic activities and semantic content [22, 25] for urban vibrancy, which can be reflected through check-in data [24]. Rich human daily activities at various locations and times, rhythms, residents' spatial and temporal preferences and interaction information can be captured with this technology [21].

In order to applying social media to measure urban vibrancy, obtained check-in records within the time and region of study are, first, pre-processed and temporal and spatial patterns of social and economic activities are extracted through check-in density distributions and accumulated on the number of people checked in. These data are then normalized to compute the strength of vibrancy resulting from the number of check-in records. Progressively, check-in hotspots are identified and mapped through visualization methods and the vibrant centres of cities are recognized based on the obtained spatial patterns. Finally, the relationship between the vibrancy and determinant factors affecting urban vibrancy are analyzed through the quantitative measures such as regression methods, Ordinary Least Squares (OLS), GWR, Geographically and Temporally Weighted Regression (GTWR) and the spatial dynamics of the analyzed factors are mapped on the urban vibrancy [21–24].

These datasets provide spatial traces of people's activities that can be connected to POI data reflecting the land use types. In addition, these are convenient enough to be received through user-friendly applications without facing privacy problems and data qualification [24]. Moreover, the social media check-in data provide a large sampling survey to characterize urban vibrancy [23]. However, there could be a risk of disclosing fallacious spatial dynamics of urban vibrancy [21] (Figure 5.4).

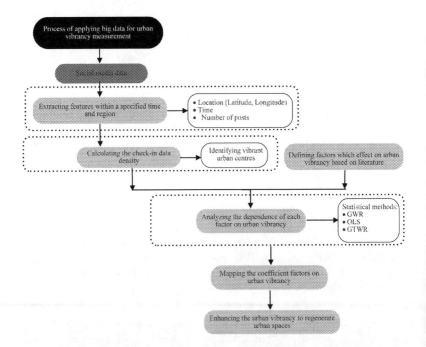

Figure 5.4 Process of social media data application in measuring urban vibrancy

Data-Centric Social Sustainability of Tehran

Bagh Ferdos[1] is one of the unique urban public spaces of Tehran (Iran's capital) which is positioned in the north of Tehran. The time of its development and use backs to more than a century ago (the Qajar dynasty) or even older. One of the most important reasons for the formation of this heritage county, same as many counties in the north of Tehran, is the mild and temperate climate and having lands suitable for gardening. Bagh Ferdos is recognized as a protected heritage place which includes open space covered with old trees, heritage buildings and a cinema museum (Figure 5.5).

As mentioned previously, a sustainable and vibrant urban public space should benefit from three main components of physical structure, meaning or imagination and activity [26]. Hence, in this section, these factors are of priority of the analysis and regeneration strategies for the case study.

Methodology and Process of Data Analysis

Data Sources

The methodology and process of the research in this chapter begins with identifying a right data source for the analysis. Among the range of various big data sources discussed in the previous sections, big data resulting from social media were chosen as the mainstream of the urban social regeneration strategies. The StatCounter database[2] was utilized to identify the most popular social media in Tehran and it was revealed that among the various social media networks including Instagram, Pinterest, Facebook, Twitter, YouTube and LinkedIn, Instagram is the most popular one (Figure 5.6). Therefore, Instagram was chosen as the big data source for the analysis of urban public space in Bagh Ferdos.

Data Processing and Analysis

The process of analysis and regeneration of Bagh Ferdos through Instagram data was done based on the following process. First, through searching the posts tagged by the Bagh Ferdos keyword (#Bagh Ferdos), 2000 posts were obtained[3] within a one-year period from 2019 to 2020. Following that, 70 posts indicating the space of Bagh Ferdos and their comments were chosen through the image caption technique and 3080 comments were retrieved. The obtained comments were pre-processed, manually labelled and 1514 related public opinion comments were extracted. Afterward, by applying content analysis and text mining methods, word frequency map and word cloud analysis were conducted by Nvivo software. For developing these items, the data were first tokenized and any URL and stop words were then

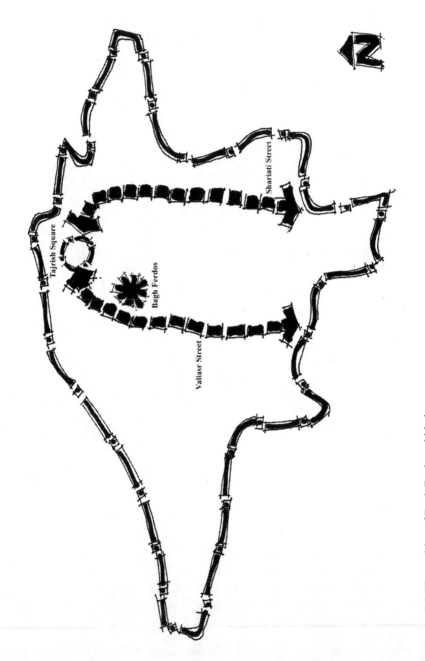

Figure 5.5 The position of Bagh Ferdos within its county

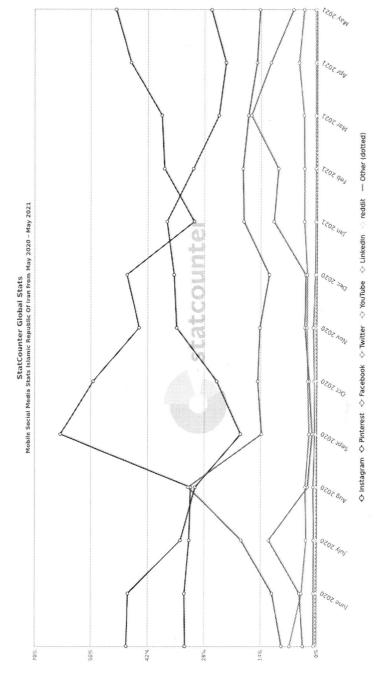

Figure 5.6 Mobile social media stats; Islamic Republic of Iran, May 2020–May 2021

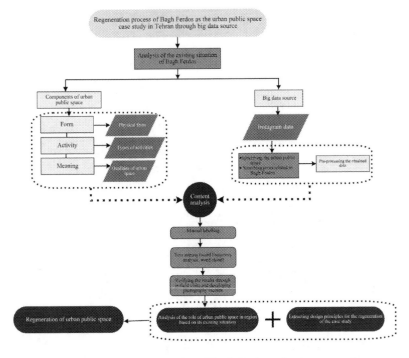

Figure 5.7 The process of regeneration of Bagh Ferdos using Instagram data

removed. The most frequently used words were further categorized into the analytical components of urban public space including physical structure, activity (function) and meaning.

Moreover, for verifying the results of the analysis and finding the suitable and target locations for the regeneration, multiple image shots were captured from the space. Meanwhile, some design principles were extracted from literature to implement as the regeneration strategies for Bagh Ferdos, based on its existing situation (Figure 5.7).

Data Analysis and Results

The main components including form, activity and meaning of Bagh Ferdos were identified via the word frequency analysis and text mining of the Instagram comments (Table 5.1).

*   Function – Activity.

Table 5.1 The word frequency analysis of Bagh Ferdos's public space components

The analyzed components for Bagh Ferdos

Physical structure	Related keywords	Freq	Activity	Related keywords	Freq	Meaning	Related keywords	Freq
Architectural form	Historical building	17	Walking	Walking	20	Positive feeling towards the space	Excellent	187
				Stepping	15			
Enclosure	Open space	2	Eating	Food	13	Sense of belonging	Memorable	35
				Café	10			
				Restaurant	10		Sense of belonging	20
				Type of food	8			
			Cultural activity	Cinema	20	Expressing beauty towards space	Beautiful	153
				Watching movie	15			
				Cinema Museum	14		Autumn	24
				Library	10			
				Photograph-photo	111		Spring	4

Activities occurring in urban public spaces establish one of the main features of urban spaces. Jan Gehl in his book, *Life Between Building* [27], classifies the activities happening in public spaces into three categories:

1) Necessary activities which are more or less compulsive such as going to school, working or shopping,
2) Optional activities when there is a desire and, time and place enable conducting these activities. These activities are performed when favourable physical and atmospheric conditions are available (Figure 5.8),
3) Social activities that rely on the attendance of others in public spaces. These activities comprise of children at playgrounds, greetings, conversations and social gatherings (Figure 5.9).

Based on the analysis of the word frequency and Instagram comments, the activities happening in Bagh Ferdos can be, mainly, classified into the optional and social types. The words and phrases mentioned by users indicate that the optional activities are mostly walking, hiking, eating food, going to a restaurant, going to a café, and doing photography. Additionally, they tend to include social activities such as going to the cinema, visiting the cinema museum, going to the public library, holding annual meetings and gathering family and friends.

Figure 5.8 Optional activities in Bagh Ferdos

Figure 5.9 Social activities in Bagh Ferdos

A holistic view on the combination of these activities indicates a great diversity, but at the same time, a great compatibility of the activities in this public space. Therefore, based on the identified patterns (social and optional), this space can be effectively transformed to the cultural-recreational centre in the north of Tehran in view of its functional opportunities.

• Meaning.

Kevin Lynch in *Good City Form* [28] delineates meaning as a feature of space which can connect a person to other aspects of life. Most objects and phenomena perceived within a space have meaning and these meanings, perceptions and their connection with residents create emotions in people. With this respect, the data analysis of Instagram comments made for Bagh Ferdos revealed the qualities such as Beauty, Ingravibility (Memorability) and Sense of belonging.

• Sense of Beauty.

Sense of Beauty is a positive feeling given to people through the perception of an aesthetic thing, process or event [29]. The analysis of Instagram

Figure 5.10 The natural landscape of Bagh Ferdos

comments indicates that most of the people have a sense of beauty toward this space because of the natural vibrancy which this space conveys. The expressed words like 'beautiful' and 'elegant' show this feeling where the users point out the beauty of its natural elements through words like 'nice autumn' and 'nice spring'. It can be, then, inferred that the beauty of this space mainly depends on the natural landscape that exits in various seasons (Figure 5.10).

• Sense of belonging (Ingravibility – Memorability).

According to Lynch (1984), the longevity of urban elements leads to solidifying users' collective memory of a space and increasing the sense of belonging towards that space [28]. The analyzed data indicates that people have a remarkable sense of belonging and memories toward Bagh Ferdos. The words and phrases such as 'having good memories', 'missing the Bagh Ferdos' and 'reminiscing the good days' in this place prove the sense of belonging and indicates that this place has Ingravibility. It further means this place has a memorable image for viewers and users.

• Physical structure (Form).

Form is a visual and clear manifestation of an urban physical structure [30]. The study indicates that people pay attention to the aesthetic forms of the located heritage buildings and their details. For example, they point out the plastering and oriental glazing of the heritage buildings of Bagh Ferdos (Figure 5.11). The degree of the enclosure is another physical structure aspect of the space. One challenge here, inferred from the comments, is that a part of Bagh Ferdos has been enclosed with fences and visitors have limited access to that (Figure 5.12). This is because the buildings within Bagh

Figure 5.11 Heritage building of Bagh Ferdos as the main physical form of the space

Figure 5.12 Fences enclosing the space

Ferdos have heritage values and should be properly conserved. But, overall, the majority commented that Bagh Ferdos is a good example of an urban open public space (Figure 5.13).

It can be concluded that Bagh Ferdos has a potential to become a vibrant and 24-hour public space which can become a cultural and recreational centre in the north of Tehran. In line with this potential, the regeneration of Bagh Ferdos can be conducted in three aspects of form, meaning and activity. The main goal of the regeneration is the reinforcement and improvement of the space compatibility (Figure 5.14).

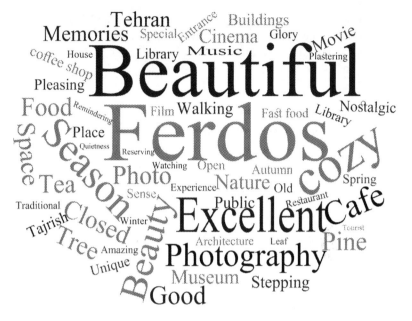

Figure 5.13 Word cloud analysis

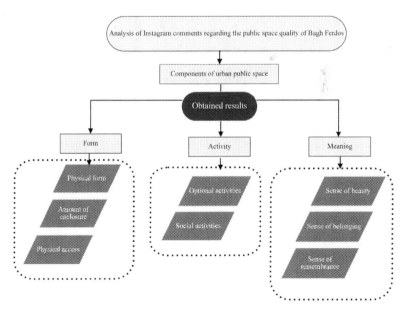

Figure 5.14 Analysis process of the Instagram comments regarding the public space quality of Bagh Ferdos

Design Principles for Regeneration of Urban Public Space

As pointed out, the design principles can be enumerated for the regeneration of an urban public space based on three main factors of form, activity and meaning. Table 5.2 indicates the identified design principles for the Bagh Ferdos space.

Table 5.2 Design principles for the regeneration of Bagh Ferdos

	Design principle	*Sketch*[1]	*Source*
Form			
	Creating connectivity between the physical body and form of urban spaces		[31]
	Keeping and preserving the physical factors that are reminiscent of collective memories and patterning valuable architectural forms		
	Creating rhythm in the physical body of urban space		
	Creating permeability and porosity in physical bodies of urban spaces		
	Predicating the space for ceremonies and festivals		

	Design principle	Sketch[1]	Source
	Residents should be able to walk around freely		[32]
Function (Activity)			
	Delivering various activities to support inclusiveness (age and gender diversity)		[33]
	Delivering active and diverse functions (24-hour activities)		[31]
	Facilitating performing different activities in one space		
	Developing harmony and compatibility between land use and activities		[34]

(Continued)

Table 5.2 (Continued)

		Design principle	Sketch[1]	Source
		Applying recreational and social activities and engagement		[32,35]
		Eliminating the incompatible land uses and activities		[31]
Meaning				
		Incorporating amenities and features for creating meaningful public spaces such as public art and sculptural furniture		[32]
		Creating a sense of safety for people through the lighting or eyes on street		[33]
		Developing social gathering and activities to enhance the sense of belonging and memory and encouraging people to more social engagement via running festivals and large-scale events		[32]

	Design principle	Sketch[1]	Source
	Conserving urban landmarks and heritage buildings for creating memorable space and improving the identity of place		[31]
	Creating spaces for people to meet up, mix and mingle for increasing the sense of belonging		
	Keeping the main name of spaces for their memorable role		

[1] Sketches are drawn by author

As mentioned before, it was realized that Bagh Ferdos is greatly potential to become a vibrant public open space. Hence, the sketch-based diagrams were developed to regenerate the space based on the design principles (Figure 5.15).

The Instagram comments indicated that this space is sometimes closed, and visitors cannot have a free access to some areas. Therefore, the fences which have environed the space should be removed to provide free access and movement for people within the public space (Figure 5.16).

The analysis also revealed that people tend to perform social gatherings and activities in this space. However, the east and west side of the space is blocked with inactive land uses and closed structures (Figure 5.17). As a result, some 24 hours and active land uses, compatible with exciting activities such as café, restaurant and handy craft shops, are proposed to enhance the vibrancy and sense of safety and belonging (Figure 5.18). Moreover,

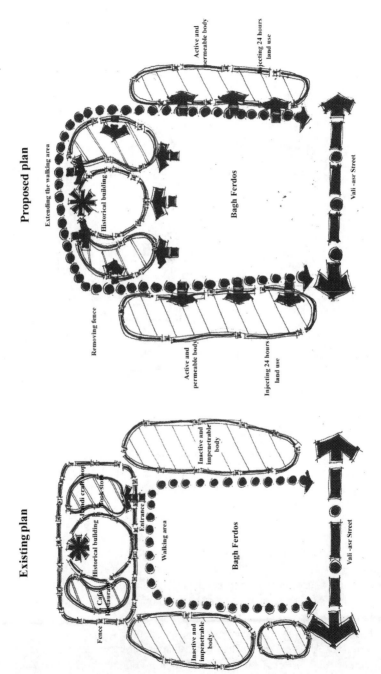

Figure 5.15 The re-design plan of Bagh Ferdos

Figure 5.16 Social regeneration of Bagh Ferdos

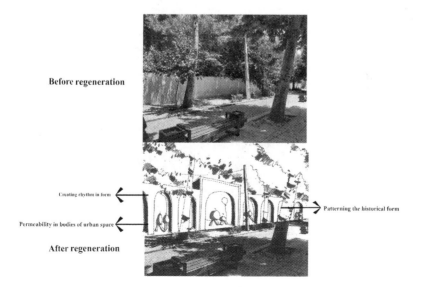

Figure 5.17 Form regeneration of the space

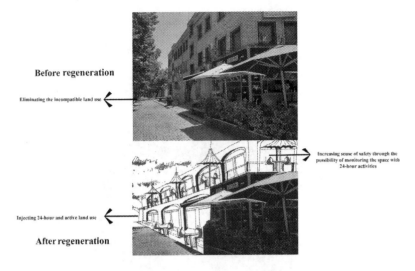

Figure 5.18 Land use activation

Figure 5.19 Sense of place development

there is some city furniture to encourage people to socialize and provide flexible spaces for performing street theatre or children's playground. All these considerations and re-design strategies can enhance the sense of place and belonging (Figure 5.19).

Furthermore, people, in their comments, pointed out to the beauty of the physical form of the heritage museum building. Hence, the architectural

Before regeneration

After regeneration

Figure 5.20 Heritage patterns application for Bagh Ferdos

form of the existing heritage building was used to pattern and apply the regenerative design strategy of the space (Figure 5.20).

It is anticipated that with the application of these changes and regenerative strategies, Bagh Ferdos can be effectively transformed to the vibrant, distinctive and high-quality urban public space. Moreover, citizens' participation and preference can be improved to provide more convenient, entertaining and comfortable space as compared to the pre-regeneration phase. Improving these qualities will also lead to enhancing the social sustainability of the space.

Conclusion

In a nutshell, it can be concluded that attractive and well-designed urban public spaces play a key role in improving the social sustainability of urban spaces. Furthermore, the analysis of these spaces through big data sources such as social media data can be much more effective and convenient for analyzing the existing situations. In fact, this method has potential to reveal the real perception of human behaviours and their mentality regarding the space in which people attend. The true status of the main components of urban spaces including form, activity and meaning are identified and characteristically deduced from social media data (Instagram comments, in this case). This information presents an effective platform for the regeneration and enhancement of the role of urban public spaces as cultural and recreational centres in modern cities.

Notes

1 Paradise Garden.
2 https://gs.statcounter.com/social-media-stats/mobile/iran
3 Instagram comments were obtained from Life Web company which deals with social media data mining. https://lifeweb.ir/

References

1 Mehan, A. and F. Soflaei, *Social sustainability in urban context: Concepts, definitions, and principles.* Architectural Research Addressing Societal Challenges Couceiro da Costa, et al. (Eds), 2017, p. 293–299.
2 Ghahramanpouri, A., H. Lamit, and S. Sedaghatnia, Urban social sustainability trends in research literature. *Asian Social Science*, 2013. 9(4): p. 185.
3 Yıldız, S., et al., Built environment design-social sustainability relation in urban renewal. *Sustainable Cities and Society*, 2020. 60: p. 102173.
4 Karuppannan, S. and A. Sivam, Social sustainability and neighbourhood design: An investigation of residents' satisfaction in Delhi. *Local Environment*, 2011. 16(9): p. 849–870.
5 Woodcraft, S., Understanding and measuring social sustainability. *Journal of Urban Regeneration & Renewal*, 2015. 8(2): p. 133–144.
6 Li, Y., et al., *A big data evaluation of urban street walkability using deep learning and environmental sensors-a case study around Osaka University Suita campus.* 2020, D2.T8.S1, The Cognitive City (AI). 2: p. 319–328.
7 Deng, C., et al., A data-driven framework for walkability measurement with open data: A case study of Triple Cities, New York. *ISPRS International Journal of Geo-Information*, 2020. 9(1): p. 36.
8 Dunn, A., B. Hanson, and C.J. Seeger, Evaluating walkability in the age of open data: OpenStreetMap and community-level transportation analysis. *Journal of Digital Landscape Architecture*, 2018. 3: p. 119–129.
9 Yamagata, Y., D. Murakami, and T. Yoshida, Evaluating walkability using mobile GPS data. In *Spatial Analysis Using Big Data*. 2020, Elsevier. p. 239–257.
10 Guan, C., M. Keith, and A. Hong, Designing walkable cities and neighborhoods in the era of urban big data. *Urban Planning International*, 2020. 34(5).
11 Karimzadeh, M., et al. Pedestrians trajectory prediction in urban environments. In *2019 International Conference on Networked Systems (NetSys)*. 2019. IEEE.
12 Ballı, S. and E.A. Sağbaş, Diagnosis of transportation modes on mobile phone using logistic regression classification. *IET Software*, 2017. 12(2): p. 142–151.
13 Lu, W., W. Yang, and T. Ai. Evaluating non-motorized transport popularity of urban roads by sports GPS tracks. In *2018 26th International Conference on Geoinformatics*. 2018. IEEE.
14 Kasemsuppakorn, P. and H.A. Karimi. Pedestrian network data collection through location-based social networks. In *2009 5th International Conference on Collaborative Computing: Networking, Applications and Worksharing*. 2009. IEEE.

15 Song, Y., J. Fernandez, and T. Wang, Understanding perceived site qualities and experiences of urban public spaces: A case study of social media reviews in Bryant park, New York city. *Sustainability*, 2020. **12**(19): p. 8036.

16 Kim, H.J., B.K. Chae, and S.B. Park, Exploring public space through social media: An exploratory case study on the High Line New York City. *Urban Design International*, 2018. **23**(2): p. 69–85.

17 Martí, P., C. García-Mayor, and L. Serrano-Estrada, Identifying opportunity places for urban regeneration through LBSNs. *Cities*, 2019. **90**: p. 191–206.

18 Agryzkov, T., et al., Analysing successful public spaces in an urban street network using data from the social networks Foursquare and Twitter. *Applied Network Science*, 2016. **1**(1): p. 1–15.

19 Zhang, L., et al., A systematic measurement of street quality through multi-sourced urban data: A human-oriented analysis. *International Journal of Environmental Research and Public Health*, 2019. **16**(10): p. 1782.

20 Huang, B., et al., Evaluating and characterizing urban vibrancy using spatial big data: Shanghai as a case study. *Environment and Planning B: Urban Analytics and City Science*, 2020. **47**(9): p. 1543–1559.

21 Tu, W., et al., Portraying the spatial dynamics of urban vibrancy using multi-source urban big data. *Computers, Environment and Urban Systems*, 2020. **80**: p. 101428.

22 Fu, R., et al., The relationship between urban vibrancy and built environment: An empirical study from an emerging city in an Arid region. *International Journal of Environmental Research and Public Health*, 2021. **18**(2): p. 525.

23 Lu, S., C. Shi, and X. Yang, Impacts of built environment on urban vitality: Regression analyses of Beijing and Chengdu, China. *International Journal of Environmental Research and Public Health*, 2019. **16**(23): p. 4592.

24 Wu, C., et al., Check-in behaviour and spatio-temporal vibrancy: An exploratory analysis in Shenzhen, China. *Cities*, 2018. **77**: p. 104–116.

25 Chen, T., et al., Identifying urban spatial structure and urban vibrancy in highly dense cities using georeferenced social media data. *Habitat International*, 2019. **89**: p. 102005.

26 Sadeghi Alireza, A.F., Perception of place components for designing the urban environment (case study: Historical piazza: Naghshe Jahan, Ganjalikhan, Del Campo, Grand Police). *Science and Technology of Environment*, 2017. **19**(NO 5): p. 559–570.

27 Gehl, J., *Life between buildings*. Vol. 23. 1987, New York: Van Nostrand Reinhold.

28 Lynch, K., *Good city form*. 1984, Massachusetts, US: MIT Press.

29 Hegel, G.W.F., *Aesthetics: Lectures on fine art*. Vol. 1. 1998, Ely House, London, UK: Oxford University Press.

30 Grutter, J.K., *Aesthetics in architecture*. Pakzad, J., Homayoun, A., 6th edition, Tehran: Shahid Beheshti University press, 1996.

31 Pakzad, J.s., *Urban spaces design guidelines in Iran*. 1386, Iran: Ministry of Housing and Urban Development, Shahidi.

32 Carmona, M., Principles for public space design, planning to do better. *Urban Design International*, 2019. **24**(1): p. 47–59.

33 Mehta, V., Evaluating public space. *Journal of Urban Design*, 2014. **19**(1): p. 53–88.

34 Bahraini, H., *Process of urban design*. 1393, Iran: University of Tehran.

35 Marcus, C.C. and C. Francis, *People places: Design guidelines for urban open space*. 1997, New York, US: John Wiley & Sons.

6 Data-Focused Visionary Leap for the Future Built Environment

Data-Integrated Pathways Towards Regenerative Urban Environments

Residents' interaction with space and time is the centric point of growth and development of urban areas but creates urban challenges, too. Hence, big data with three main attributes –velocity, variety and value – and three types of voluntary, automatic and monitored datasets can be effectively applied for understanding patterns, flows and behaviours of citizens. Big data sources lead to the sustainable urban regeneration and resolution of urban issues based on the profound perception of human patterns including human activities, mobilities, behaviour and impacts in real time.

With this respect, it was identified that urban functions and land uses are one of the main elements of configuring the form of cities. Understanding how urban functions are distributed is imperative for sustainable land use planning and its regeneration. Therefore, the urban land use regeneration study was conducted in Beijing for three types of educational, medical and green spaces using voluntary, social media (Sina Weibo check-in) and POI datasets. Based on these big datasets, the existing situation for the distribution of primary school, hospital and green space land uses were obtained as the basis for their regeneration. Following this step, the land suitability analysis was applied and the AHP technique was employed to propose the new areas for positioning the primary school, hospital and green space land uses for residential regions to alleviate the shortage of these critical infrastructures and enhance the sustainability of the impacted regions.

As to the urban transportation infrastructures, it was discussed that the travel behaviour analysis and mobility patterns are the essential components for any sustainable urban transportation and regenerative planning. Therefore, as discussed in Chapter 3, the travel pattern analysis was performed for Beijing based on the taxi GPS trajectories and their coincidental data correlation with taxi mobilities. Through the space-time cube analysis

DOI: 10.4324/9781003139942-6

with taxi GPS points as the input, hotspot and cold spot areas were specified in the spatial scale for a one-week period. Based on the obtained transportation patterns, the design solutions were proposed for the reinforcement of metro networks, transforming the monocentric spatial structures to polycentric ones, restrictions on commuting of private cars in hotspot regions and more development of the green transportation modes in hotspot areas.

The next data-integrated pathway was taken to realize the environmental footprints including air and noise pollution and their role in urban regeneration. Tehran's urban air pollution was, hence, analyzed based on the automatic big data sources. Through the fixed stations which monitor pollution in real time, geographical distribution and dispersion of PM 2.5 pollutant was calculated and the hotspot concentration areas of this pollutant were obtained. In parallel, through the GWR, the relationship between the urban planning factors including land use, physical form, urban vegetation and transportation with the pollutant amount was also surveyed. Finally, based on the design principles and analysis of urban planning factors influencing air pollution intensity, urban regeneration interventions, including land use, vegetation, transportation and physical form, were applied in the hotspot areas to reduce air pollution and improve the environmental states.

Finally, it was identified that social sustainability, as the essential element of a sustainable city, can be enhanced through the physical factors such as attractive and well-designed urban public spaces. The last data-driven pathway was, then, focused on the social regeneration of Bagh Ferdos, as one of the urban public spaces located in the north of Tehran. This project was performed using social media data and Instagram comments as the voluntary big data source. Text mining methods (word frequency and word cloud analyses) were applied on residents' Instagram comments on the existing situation of Bagh Ferdos in three aspects of form, activity and meaning. Based on the results and their verifications through photography and imaging techniques, design solutions, including plan and form regeneration, land use activation, sense of place development and heritage design patterns, were applied to enhance the space, eliminate imperfections and develop the more vibrant public space (Figure 6.1).

Case Studies and Knowledge Factors

The key processes and findings of the urban regeneration in four aspects of land use, traffic and transportation, environmental and social showed that big data objectives were applied successfully and satisfactorily. Achieving these objectives entails the lessons learned and knowledge factors as discussed next.

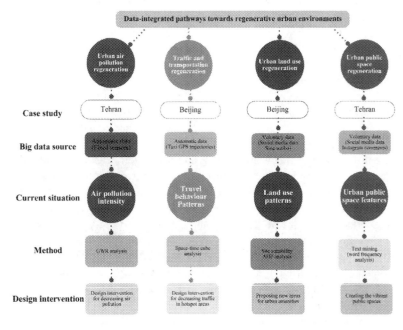

Figure 6.1 Data-integrated pathways towards regenerative urban environments

Beijing's Urban Land Use Regeneration

The land suitability analysis for predicting urban services including educational, green space and healthcare infrastructures of Beijing was done through the Sina Weibo big data. These types of data help discovering the land use patterns much more conveniently in comparison with the manual methods. The analysis with this big data source delivered the following features about functional attributes of Beijing:

- Functional structure of the city was specified,
- The regions covered with urban amenities were identified,
- The regions which require urban services were determined,
- The suitable and unsuitable lands for locating new urban services were discovered,
- The distribution mode of urban services was determined.

Therefore, the application of the human-centric big data for the urban land use regeneration was proven in proposing new urban services.

Beijing's Traffic and Transportation Regeneration

Discovering travel behaviour patterns is one of the main important sources for the urban transportation regeneration process. By analyzing Beijing's traffic and transportation networks with taxi GPS datasets, the main features of the city were identified:

* The monocentric spatial structure of the city was discovered,
* The hotspot regions which attract travels were specified,
* The spatial and temporal patterns were analyzed,
* The functional structures such as official and commercial concentration areas were identified,
* The regions which require the investment on their transportation infrastructures (green and public) were identified.

These elements of the analysis and knowledge factors created a detailed traffic understanding of Beijing and paved the way for its planning and design regeneration.

Tehran's Urban Air Pollution Regeneration

As to Tehran's serious environmental problem and its PM 2.5 pollutant intensity, big data-based pollution analysis revealed that the concentration of pollution is different from one point to another point due to the factors such as land use, physical form, urban vegetation and transportation. Thus, by applying GWR technique, the correlation between urban planning factors with pollution concentration was effectively recognized. It was proven that the intensity of air pollution in various urban areas is different because of these factors' impacts. For instance, in some regions of Tehran, green space areas have an effective role to decrease the air pollution. However, there are some other regions having green space areas that are adjacent to industrial land uses and are heavily influenced by the high level of air pollution.

Accordingly, Tehran's urban areas were regenerated through the redesign or improvement of the following affecting factors:

* The redesign of physical forms such as changing the height of buildings and creating porosity in urban blocks,
* Development of green transportation infrastructures,
* Green space development and expansions,
* Transferring polluting activities to non-urban areas.

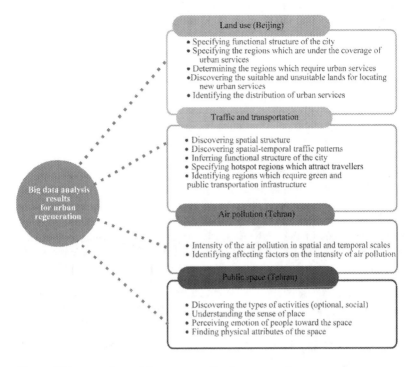

Figure 6.2 Lessons learned from case studies for regeneration process

Tehran's Urban Public Space Regeneration

As discussed in the previous chapter, a well-designed urban public space can contribute to the urban social sustainability. The regeneration of Tehran's urban public space was studied through applying social media data in identifying the main components of form, activity and meaning in its original situation. It was, hence, realized that the main attributes for this part consist of:

- The social, physical and recreational activities which happen in the space,
- The sense of place and emotions of people toward the space,
- The physical attributes of the space.

It was inferred that the developed analysis provides a reliable basis to understand the real perception of users of the space and regenerate it based on the obtained information (Figure 6.2).

Challenges, Implications and Visions

Challenges

There are, however, obvious challenges for regenerating urban environments through big data technology. Finding a proper big data source and getting access are the main difficulties with this respect. These difficulties lie in the security and privacy of these types of data and their high prices. Consequently, individuals and freelance researchers have a challenge in the access to and analysis of big data for urban analytics.

The next issue is linked to the context of the research and case study analysis. Finding these types of data for the analysis of cities located in developing countries, such as Iran, is a daunting task. This is due to the low maturity of the digital transformation level and smart cities' integration in the urban structures of developing countries.

Moreover, the in-depth analysis of these datasets requires a multidisciplinary team of experts collaborating with urban planners and designers to identify the spatial and temporal patterns of data. Therefore, it is of significance to find professional experts of data science for precise analysis. Hence, it can be said that the acquisition, storage, management and analysis of big data are substantial challenges for the data-driven regeneration of urban environments.

Another challenge can be presented from the methodological point of view. Big data analysis is an objective technique, requiring deductive approach and falls to the quantitative method. On the other hand, urban design solutions are generally subjective, inductive and relevant to enhancing the quality of urban environments and mostly fall to qualitative methods. Therefore, finding a suitable approach to create a proper connection between the quantitative analysis of urban big data with the qualitative design solutions can be a challenge for this area of research.

Implications

In spite of the challenges, the data-centric urban regeneration of land use, traffic and transportation, environmental pollutions and public spaces delivers highly effective outcomes towards sustainable urban development.

The regeneration of urban land uses and traffic and transportation networks using human-centric data can lead to a fairer distribution of urban services and infrastructures, instead of having them concentrated in dense or developed regions. This will, subsequently, deliver a balanced growth, development and equity of social and economic opportunities across the boundary of a city. The access to various transportation modes may result in the enhanced use of public and green (e.g., bicycle) transportation services, as the sustainable alternatives for personal cars. Moreover, finding the traffic patterns and hotspot areas assist authorities to allocate the funding and investment on transportation infrastructures towards the regions which are in genuine need. These implications will collectively lead to not only resolving urban traffic and pollution issues, but also delivering more sustainable cities.

Tehran's urban air pollution regeneration induces more environmental sustainability. Evidently, urban pollution reduction enhances both physical and mental health of residents which, in turn, delivers significant social and economic benefits for the public and community. These benefits can be integrated with more comprehensive analysis of urban public space components (form, activity and meaning) from the perspective of residents and create more vibrant public spaces. Social interactions and social cohesion of people in urban spaces will be, thus, strengthened, leading to urban social sustainability.

Visions

With the progressive maturity of big data technology and its complete integration with AI, it is anticipated that urban issues can be greatly alleviated through human-centric and real-time data. This is where residents of a city are considered as the real users of urban areas and act as the live sensors for revealing urban issues. In other words, people will directly and/or indirectly collaborate in urban issues resolution. It is anticipated that these processes could be done in a shorter period of time (minutes/hours/days) rather than longer periods (years/decades), and unforeseen quantitative, qualitative and longitudinal relationships can be properly identified.

Moreover, the hidden layers of urban spaces and urban problems can be revealed through big data sources which cannot be perceived via traditional data sources. Getting access to big datasets facilitates more precise quantitative analysis and in-depth spatial and temporal investigations. It is also expected that with the current technology improvements in the acquisition and analytical methods of big data, more urban experts in different fields (traffic and transportation, environmental, economic and social structures) and different contexts (developed and developing economies) apply this technology and make real-time decisions for urban planning and design projects.

Index

174   *Index*

improved density-based clustering application (IDBSCAN) 24
Instagram: comments, analysis process *155*; data, usage *150*; usage 5
intra-urban transportation, efficiency/ functionality 71
Islamic Republic of Iran, mobile social media data *149*

k-means 24, 25
k-medoids 24
knowledge factors 167–170

land: scarcity, anthropogenic pressures/ urbanization growth (impact) 20; use, types (geo-tagged social media check-in data benefit) 26
landmark areas, photos 24
land suitability analysis *50*; criteria *40, 41*
land use map, accuracy (validation) 24
land use patterns: data-centric land use patterns 22–28; identification process, taxi GPS data/social media data/MPD (usage) *29*; investigation, MPD usage (advantages) 27; recognition, data collection methods *23*
land use types, identification 26
Laney, Doug 3
lexicon-based sentiment analysis 143
Life Between Building (Gehl) 151
location-based service (LBS) 7
location-based social media data 5
Lynch, Kevin 152

machine learning algorithms, usage 96
Markov Random Field, usage 96
Mashey, John 2
metro networks, expansion 78
mobile phone applications: attributes *103*; benefits/challenges 101; usage 99–101
mobile phone data (MPD) 5, 7, 22, 26–28; application, challenges 27; technology, usage 27; usage *29*; usage, advantages 27
mobile social media, data (Islamic Republic of Iran) *149*
monitored data 8–9
monocentric spatial structure, shift 78
Municipality of Tehran, air pollution reduction 104

Natural Language Processing (NLP) 96
network analysis, usage 143
nitric oxide (NO) emissions 139
noise levels: geographical coordinates 100; tagging (geographical coordinates), GPS receivers (usage) 100
noise monitoring: mobile phone applications, usage 99–101; wireless sensor networks (WSNs), usage 102
noise pollution, impact 98–99
noise pollution monitoring: mobile phone applications/WSNs, attributes *103*; process, big data sources (usage) *103*
NoiseSPY (app), usage 99
Noise Tube (app), usage 99
Nvivo software 147

OD flow, chord diagram sample *68*
OD matrix 66; sample *67*
Open Door Policy 28
open street map (OSM): road network 31, 59; usage 33
Ordinary Kriging, usage 106
Ordinary Least Squares (OLS), usage 146
origin-destinations 65

Pearson correlation coefficient, usage 96
pick-up/drop-off points 23
planning approach, urban environmental issues/impacts 92–93
PM 2.5 pollutant, concern (Tehran) 104
Point of Interest (POI) data 24–25, 30–31, 146
private car commutes, restricted areas *85*
private sector data 9
public spaces, activities (classification) 151

regeneration: application 2; processes, case studies lessons *170*
regenerative urban environments, data-integrated pathways (usage) 166–167, *168*
regression: analysis, usage 140; methods 146

self-organizing maps (SOM) 25
sensors/objects, usage 7–8

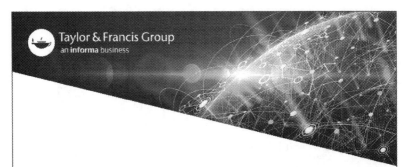

Printed in the United States
by Baker & Taylor Publisher Services